THE ULTIMATE NEW YORK METS
TIME MACHINE BOOK

THE ULTIMATE NEW YORK METS TIME MACHINE BOOK

MARTIN GITLIN

Guilford, Connecticut

An imprint of The Rowman & Littlefield Publishing Group, Inc.
4501 Forbes Blvd., Ste. 200
Lanham, MD 20706
www.rowman.com

Distributed by NATIONAL BOOK NETWORK

British Library Cataloguing in Publication Information available

Library of Congress Control Number: 2020950571

ISBN 978-1-4930-5532-6 (paperback)
ISBN 978-1-4930-5533-3 (e-book)

♾™ The paper used in this publication meets the minimum requirements of American National Standard for Information Sciences—Permanence of Paper for Printed Library Materials, ANSI/NISO Z39.48-1992.

CONTENTS

Introduction VII

CHAPTER 1: Conception and Birth in the Big Apple 1
CHAPTER 2: The Worst Darn Team in History 8
CHAPTER 3: Oh Shea Can You See 15
CHAPTER 4: Tom Terrific 23
CHAPTER 5: From Chumps to Champs 33
CHAPTER 6: Yogi and the Years of Mediocrity 43
CHAPTER 7: From Contention to Collapse 52
CHAPTER 8: The Kiddie Corps 60
CHAPTER 9: Fighting Greatness 71
CHAPTER 10: 1986 80
CHAPTER 11: When Great Was Not Good Enough 94
CHAPTER 12: Goodbye Davey, Hello Misery 104
CHAPTER 13: The Hometown Closer 111
CHAPTER 14: Valentine's Day 119
CHAPTER 15: Super Season 131
CHAPTER 16: The Subway Series 139
CHAPTER 17: The End of Valentine's Day—and Howe 150
CHAPTER 18: It's All Wright 158
CHAPTER 19: New Manager, New GM, New Park in New York . . 169
CHAPTER 20: New Home, Bad Baseball, and a Surprise 181
CHAPTER 21: The Sky Fell 192

Notes 199

INTRODUCTION

I NEVER QUESTIONED MY BASEBALL FANDOM AS A CHILD OF THE SIXTIES. I was simply ignorant. Though young people of that era felt a far greater appreciation and love for what was then still fully accepted as the national pastime, they were also more provincial in their sports passions. I loved my hometown Cleveland Indians and was never driven to study the travails of other major-league franchises.

The expansion of such knowledge was difficult in those days. Coverage was virtually all local, aside from weekly sports print magazines. The only national exposure to baseball action in the regular season was *The Saturday Game of the Week*. There was no ESPN, no MLB Network. There was no internet on which to cultivate interest beyond the area team. Sportscasters and sportswriters spewed out little information about different clubs. And there was no interleague play.

I, therefore, had not grasped the notion as a kid that passionate baseball fans gained information about other teams through the study of box scores and national publications. I knew little about the New York Mets, especially since they competed in the National League and never paid a visit to decrepit Municipal Stadium. But I did know this:

They stunk—and they seemed destined to stink heading into each season.

The Mets finished last or second-to-last every year from 1962 to 1968. They exceeded 100 defeats five times during that stretch. But what I did not realize was the adoration Mets fans felt for their hapless club. New Yorkers embraced them as lovable losers, the opposite of a Yankees team that had remained a dynasty through the first three years of the Mets' existence. Fans felt both empathy and sympathy for the downtrodden Mets. Marvelous Marv Throneberry would drop another popup. It didn't matter. Casey Stengel would snooze on the bench. It didn't matter. Choo-Choo Coleman would allow yet another passed ball to scoot to the backstop. It didn't matter. The fans still besieged the ballpark to cheer the Mets.

The result was that the team ranked between second and fourth in National League attendance every season between 1963 and 1968. Nearly two million patrons streamed through the gates annually at brand-spanking-new Shea Stadium to watch the worst darn team in baseball. Impressive given that many teams, including my beloved Indians, usually failed to even attract one million.

The Mets had been sneaking up on their National League brethren by early 1968 with a rotation spearheaded by the brilliance of young Tom Seaver, rookie southpaw Jerry Koosman, and flame-throwing future Hall of Famer Nolan Ryan. Even the 11-year-old following the exploits of the Indians in Cleveland devoured a *Sports Illustrated* article in May of that year spotlighting the staff stifling hitters at Shea as the Year of the Pitcher unfolded.

Then it happened. Few believed the Mets were on the precipice of greatness after a second-half collapse in 1968. Perhaps the .500 record through June that season indicated that the Mets were coming. But who expected them to take baseball by storm in 1969? Perhaps the most memorable and remarkable single-season rise in American sports history began with little indication that the team could transform itself from also-ran to champion. And even when the Mets finally emerged as a winner, the prospect of an October celebration seemed unthinkable. Their crisscross of the Cubs in the first National League Eastern Division standings in September boggled the mind and focused the attention of sports fans not just on the likes of Seaver and Koosman but also on budding position-player standouts such as Cleon Jones and Tommie Agee. They were all becoming household names. And when they reveled in their pennant and the unlikely upset victory over powerful Baltimore in the World Series, America rejoiced along with them. They had become the darlings of baseball.

One could never claim about any franchise that its rich history began with seven seasons of last-place or second-to-last finishes. But the comical ineptitude of the early teams and the level to which they were embraced by fans only adds to the historical richness of the franchise. And it makes the Miracle Mets of 1969 that much more of a miracle.

The *Ultimate New York Mets Time Machine Book* will track that rich history from the bungling band of the early 1960s to the mediocrity, and then the collapse of the 1970s and early 1980s to the rebirth and a championship under Davey Johnson to the bad contracts (Bobby Bonilla!) through to the wildly inconsistent and periodically powerful teams of the current generation. It will delve into the greatest and most intriguing players, teams, and events in Mets' lore.

This book explores the history of a club forever known for its starting pitching from Seaver and Koosman to Jon Matlack to Dwight Gooden to Jacob deGrom. It delves into the struggles of developing and also keeping consistently potent hitters beyond the likes of Darryl Strawberry, Mike Piazza, and David Wright. It details the imbalance in free-agent success—the horrors of Bonilla and Óliver Pérez and Vince Coleman and Jason Bay far outweighing the triumphs of Carlos Beltrán and Robin Ventura. And it highlights the highs and lows of managerial experiences from the sleeping Stengel to the pre-Yankees failures of a young Joe Torre to the shrewd sharpness of Johnson to the ups and downs of Bobby Valentine and Terry Collins to the quickly dispatched Mickey Callaway.

It's all here—the good, the bad, and the ugly. Enjoy.

CHAPTER ONE

Conception and Birth in the Big Apple

THE GAPING HOLE REMAINED IN THE HEARTS OF MILLIONS OF NEW York baseball fans. The one-two punch still had them reeling. On May 28, 1957, the National League voted unanimously to allow Dodgers owner Walter O'Malley to move the team to Los Angeles and Giants counterpart Horace Stoneham to take his club from Manhattan to San Francisco. The lone franchise remaining in New York was the Yankees, whom many in America's largest city and certainly beyond perceived as the "Evil Empire."

Mayor Robert Wagner, who was seeking reelection for a second term and would eventually win a third, elicited the help of attorney William Shea, a protégé of banker George McLaughlin, the guardian of the Dodgers' trust under Charles Ebbets, for whom Ebbets Field had been named. Wagner appointed Shea the head of a committee of four to bring another team to New York. Shea attempted to lure an existing franchise to no avail. The Reds, Phillies, and Pirates all rejected his offers.

The result was a conception but not a birth. Shea proposed a new venture that was eventually tossed into the dustbin of baseball history called the Continental League, which would have been the first rival to Major League Baseball since the Federal League of 1913 to 1915. Its main purpose was to counteract the loss of the Dodgers and Giants by launching a new club in the Big Apple. Legendary baseball executive Branch Rickey, who had ended the shameful practice of segregation twelve years earlier by signing Jackie Robinson to a Dodgers contract, provided immediate credibility for the new circuit by agreeing to serve as its president after leaving the same position with Pittsburgh.

The Continental League of Professional Baseball Clubs (CL) was officially announced in late July 1959 with plans for the first pitch in April 1961. Franchises were also established for Houston, Minneapolis-St. Paul, Toronto, Denver, and, eventually, Atlanta, Dallas-Fort Worth, and Buffalo, all of which, aside from the latter, would eventually land MLB teams.

The competition, especially in New York, alarmed Major League Baseball. So, on July 18, 1960, the MLB announced what amounted to its first-ever expansion. Both the American and National Leagues had consisted of eight teams since the former launched into existence in 1901. Many believed the growth of dozens of cities warranted the addition of new clubs anyway. Therefore, the Los Angeles Angels and Washington Senators, who replaced the team with the same name that had moved to Minneapolis-St. Paul, joined the American League in 1961. And the Houston Colt .45s and New York Mets entered the National League in 1962.

The Metropolitan Baseball Club of New York was officially born, and the Continental League was officially dead. The new franchise issued the following statement, expressing its joy over a decision of the National League that reignited the fandom of those that once followed the Dodgers and Giants:

> We accept this as an obligation to baseball followers the world over, to organized baseball, to the National League and particularly to the people of the New York metropolitan area whose support we are confident we will earn. We are well aware of the National League's outstanding history in New York, and that a tremendous task lies ahead.[1]

Those tasks fell into the lap of Joan Whitney Payson, who had been a 10 percent stockholder of the Giants and attempted in vain to keep that team in New York. Shea had selected Payson to head an ownership group for the proposed Continental League team. She, therefore, became the natural choice to head the Mets, though she had preferred naming the new club the Meadowlarks. Payson emerged as the third woman ever to own an MLB franchise and first in over four decades.

The Mets appeared on solid ground in the front office. They named as general manager none other than George Weiss, a figure familiar to New York baseball fans as the prime architect of the post-Babe Ruth Yankees dynasty. Weiss had served as their farm director from 1932 to 1946 before taking over as GM. His skills as a talent evaluator had been unquestioned. Few could have forgotten that Weiss boasted the guts and intuition to hire an aging Casey Stengel as manager of the Bronx Bombers in 1949. That roundly criticized move was lauded as being genius after Stengel guided his team to ten pennants and seven World Series titles in twelve years. The Yankees fired him after a seven-game defeat by Pittsburgh in the 1960 Fall Classic, marking a second straight season without a Series crown, a positively ghastly development for the most dominant team in American sports.

Stengel was down but not out. Despite having turned seventy, he remained a hot commodity. He nixed several managerial offers, including one from the Detroit Tigers. He even at first rejected an opportunity from Weiss to return to New York. But the GM remained persistent. He yearned to bring a familiar name with a history of success to the new team and eventually convinced Stengel to accept the job. The Mets stole some thunder from the Yankees before the opening of the 1961 World Series by announcing that Stengel had been hired as their first manager.

Among the first missions of the fledgling franchise was settling on a home. O'Malley, who had balked at the Angels invading his territory in Los Angeles, suggested the Mets share Yankee Stadium for one season, but Yankees president Dan Topping had stated he would only agree to a long-range commitment. O'Malley then revealed he had spoken with Stoneham, who suggested the Mets play at the Polo Grounds, former home of the Giants. Such was not an ideal solution—that dilapidated park was more than eighty years old and among the reasons its team had bolted for the West Coast. O'Malley had even heard that it would soon be condemned for housing.

The Mets had little choice. The Polo Grounds proved their only viable option. Making matters worse was that the turf was already being

The lineup card produced by Mets first manager Casey Stengel boasted players who were a far cry in talent than those he managed with the Yankees.

ground up by the American Football League New York Titans (later renamed the Jets). The seats were shabby and filthy, the ironwork a sickly green. Titans owner Harry Wismer deemed it a "graveyard." The Mets spent $350,000 to paint the inside a brighter green, add the team's orange and blue colors to the outside, install new lights, and cover some of the dinginess with ads along the outfield walls. But those improvements were more akin to lipstick on a pig than reconstructive surgery. Legendary *New York Herald Tribune* sportswriter Red Smith offered that the 400-seat lounge under the stands would prove prudent. "Watching the Mets on the field may very well drive fans to drink," he explained.[2]

Wagner had required a more concrete plan to house the Mets before he could convince National League owners to vote in favor of adding the new club. He informed them of a proposal to construct a 55,000-seat stadium at Flushing Meadows Park but that it would not be set to host major-league games by the start of the 1962 season. Far from it—groundbreaking at the Queens site did not occur until the cold, blustery morning of October 28, 1961. That bit of news did not deter the group from accepting the Mets, who nevertheless felt a sense of urgency to build a permanent home. The original name was Flushing Meadows Stadium, but civic leader Bernard Gimbel led an effort to honor the man whose drive made the Mets a reality. It would be known instead as Shea Stadium.

The Mets had already planted the seeds for their futility. Nearly three weeks previous to the first shovel striking dirt, they had butchered the expansion draft. The 67-year-old Weiss set out to prove to the Yankees that he remained spry enough to construct a strong club. He then failed spectacularly. Rather than plucking almost-exclusively younger players from the rosters of their new National League brethren with the understanding that building a winner takes time, they sought to gain immediate respectability by selecting several veterans in the twilights of their careers.

Not that a dazzling array of future all-stars were there for the taking. Major League Baseball required each club to make 15 players available from the 40-man rosters, seven from the 25-man rosters as they were constructed on August 31, 1961. So, clubs purposely altered them for

The Mets finally had their first real home when Shea Stadium opened in 1964.
© FFOOTER/DREAMSTIME

the game that day to ensure their top prospects would not be exposed. "I figured the list of players would be bad," complained Houston general manager Paul Richards. "But they're worse than I thought they'd be."[3]

And the Mets maximized their potential for disaster. Some choices were downright laughable, such as 31-year-old backup catcher Hobie Landrith, whose claim to fame was managing to remain in the big leagues since 1950 despite only twice playing in more than 100 games in a season. Weiss inexplicably targeted Landrith as their top choice as Stengel explained the need to prevent passed balls from careening to backstops. Landrith played just one month for the Mets before being dispatched to Baltimore as the player to be named later in the trade that brought folk hero Marvelous Marv Throneberry to New York.

The pick of Landrith was far from the only head-scratcher. The Mets sought to bring familiar faces back, even if their baseball careers had one foot on a banana peel and the other in a grave. They selected eight-time all-star first baseman and outfielder Gil Hodges, a Brooklyn Dodgers standout who was set to turn 38 years old when the 1962 Mets took the field. Hodges would, of course, return to play hero in a much different role. They also plucked outfielder Gus Bell, who had faded badly with Cincinnati after hitting the big 3-0 three years earlier. Many of the other picks were simply flops, including second-selection Elio Chacón, a powerless middle infielder who never spent another day in the big leagues after serving as a decent part-time starter with the Mets in 1962.

The obstacles facing expansion clubs are steep enough. Established franchises do not leave their premier major-league and minor-league talent unprotected. Free agency was merely a twinkle in Marvin Miller's eye back in 1961. Expansion teams had yet to groom players in their farm systems. There is a reason none has ever lost fewer than 91 games in their first season. But the Mets did themselves no favors in the draft, which builds the foundation for a roster for years to come. They placed themselves in a hole so deep that it proved impossible to climb out for the foreseeable future.

CHAPTER TWO

The Worst Darn Team in History

FEW ASIDE FROM THOSE WEARING PRESCRIPTION ROSE-COLORED glasses denied that as the 1962 Mets arrived at spring training in St. Petersburg, Florida, they would struggle. But nobody could have imagined the level of futility the team would display in that first season and beyond.

Casey Stengel proved an ideal choice as manager to draw attention away from the folly on the field and lighten its impact on fans and the media. The eminently quotable quipster, who embraced the nickname "Ol' Perfessor," worked tirelessly with the younger players but also engaged in a running commentary with fans and media members, including those to whom he insisted print his demand that players abstain from sex all season—as if young ballplayers married or unmarried were not going to find a way.

Stengel provided even more levity than usual that spring by agreeing to star in a television commercial for Bromo-Seltzer in which he argued so vociferously with an umpire that he needed to calm his raging stomach. Asked beforehand if he actually took Bromo-Seltzer—the FCC was beginning to frown upon those who endorsed products they did not use—Stengel replied that he did but actually didn't because he never got sick. He then overacted by clutching his stomach like it was about to explode, prompting criticism from the director. "You mean you don't want me to die?" Stengel asked. "I'm old enough." The manager then seemed to forget the product altogether after filming, bragging the next few weeks about how he had promoted Alka-Seltzer.[1]

The Mets embarked immediately on their path to "Lovable Loser Land." Among the humorous stories, there was one that revolved around a laughably hopeful 21-year-old named John Pappas, an Astoria native with no organized baseball experience who wandered uninvited into camp with a canvas bag and a dream. At 5-foot-10 and 150 pounds, he proclaimed himself ready to display his wicked-fast fastball to assistant general manager John Murphy. Murphy did not allow Pappas to work out with the club, opting instead to accompany him to a nearby high school field. The prospect of a Horatio Alger story come to life intrigued media members who tagged along until Pappas unleashed pitches that even Mets hitters could have smashed into orbit if they had traveled miraculously near the strike zone. Pappas remained undaunted after his unceremonious dismissal from the premises—he told a sportswriter that he also played the outfield.[2]

He might not have performed all that much worse on the mound than did projected rotation standout Jay Hook against Baltimore in his last exhibition start. Hook, an engineering student at Northwestern and member of the National Rocket Society who nevertheless deemed the Roger Maris feat of hitting 61 home runs in 1961 more impressive than John Glenn's three orbits of the Earth, was kept in the game by Stengel despite allowing 17 hits. By then, Stengel had already exhibited his sadistic side in February when he featured two of his worst rookies—Dawes Hamilt and Bruce Fitzpatrick—as the faces of the franchise at a press conference. Their photos were splashed across the seven New York daily newspapers. Then they were waived.

Not that the Mets were forecast for oblivion heading into the regular season. They finished spring training with a respectable 12-15 record. Some in the media predicted a middle-of-the-pack finish, even as high as third place in the 10-team National League. The presence of veteran standouts such as Gus Bell, Gil Hodges, and Richie Ashburn inspired optimism, never mind that one and all were nearing the end of their illustrious careers. The wholly unrealistic notion of replacing the departed Giants and Dodgers in New York with a team that could compete against them crept into the media landscape. Optimism always reigns among major league baseball teams in the spring. The realism of such hope varies

Jay Hook could explain a curveball in scientific terms and did earn the first victory in franchise history but was out of baseball by 1964.

based on individual talent and career paths. That the Mets could even be mediocre seems silly in retrospect.

And they wasted no time proving it. They debuted with a three-error debacle in an 11-4 defeat in St. Louis, then lost eight in a row to tie a National League record for futility to begin a season before Hook, who had outperformed his fellow starters early in the year, pitched them to their first-ever victory against the unbeaten Pirates. Incredibly and somewhat humorously to the growing legion of Mets fans who had begun to embrace their ineptitude, and to baseball followers around the country, they had fallen nine-and-a-half games out of first place despite having played just nine games. It was no wonder—they were allowing nearly eight runs per game and had scored more than four just once.

Some performances were indeed comical. In an 11-9 loss to Philadelphia four days after their first triumph, second baseman Charlie Neal blew two routine plays that a benevolent official scorer did not mark as errors, left fielder Frank Thomas dropped an easy popup, confusion ensued on a ground ball leaving nobody to cover first base, and Hobie Landrith, the catcher whom the Mets selected first in the expansion draft because Stengel railed against passed balls, was charged with two passed balls.

But fans soon had reason to believe, to paraphrase Mark Twain, that reports of the 1962 Mets' death were greatly exaggerated. The team suddenly warmed with the weather, winning nine of 12. They beat the Cubs three of three. And they finished their run by taking three straight in Milwaukee, home of future Hall of Famers Hank Aaron and Eddie Mathews. Included was a doubleheader sweep in which the Mets scored 16 runs.

One could justify optimism that Weiss had built a roster that could at least thrive offensively. Center fielder Jim Hickman boasted a .387 on-base percentage and was on pace to score nearly 100 runs for the season. Shortstop Elio Chacon, on whom the club had pinned high hopes, managed to slam 13 hits over an eight-game period. Third baseman Felix Mantilla was batting .313 and had completed a 14-game hitting streak. Thomas had already slammed 10 home runs and was in the midst of an 18-game hitting streak. Second baseman Charlie Neal was on pace for 80 runs batted in.

Then it happened: the collapse. Or, rather, "The Collapse." A 17-game losing streak that signaled this was no ordinary struggling expansion team. The Mets were outscored 110-54 during that skein. Most embarrassing was an 11-game stretch in which they allowed 93 runs against the Giants and Dodgers clubs they had replaced in the hearts and minds of New York fans. The Mets flopped at the Polo Grounds against those two teams in five home dates, including two doubleheaders, for which they averaged more than 39,000 patrons.

The most notable personnel move was the installation by Stengel of the immortal Marvelous Marv Throneberry as the starting first baseman. Acquired on May 9 from Baltimore for a player to be named later, which proved to be Landrith, the man with a penchant for power emerged as the poster child for the team's numbing ineptitude. His stone hands afield and gaffes on the basepaths more than negated the positive effect of his occasional home run and brought comical relief to daily defeats. Usually forgiving Mets fans booed him unmercifully.

Even his hits proved problematic. The funniest, or saddest (depending on the point of view), occurred in the first game of a doubleheader at the Polo Grounds against the Cubs on June 17. Throneberry began the proceedings ignominiously when he was called for interference in the top of the first. He appeared to have made up for the mistake in the bottom of the inning when he hit a triple. But veteran umpire Dusty Boggess called him out for failing to step on second base. When Stengel stormed out of the dugout to dispute the decision, Boggess reacted swiftly. "Don't bother arguing, Casey," stressed the ump. "He missed first base, too."[3] The blunder cost the Mets a run and possibly a win when Neal followed with a home run, and the Cubs went on to an 8-7 victory.

Throneberry, who committed a whopping 17 errors in just 97 games with the 1962 Mets, became angry at the catcalls at the Polo Grounds. But he eventually grew to accept his place as the fall guy for the lousiest team in baseball history. After one typically galling individual performance in yet another defeat, he sat in the clubhouse next to Ashburn with rain dripping monotonously from a leaky ceiling onto his balding head. "I deserve it," he stated plainly to his teammate. "Yes, you do," replied Ashburn.[4]

The Mets could not recover from their epic May slide. They never won consecutive games from June 10 to August 4. They lost 16 of 17 in July. They dropped 13 straight in August. They finished the season on a 6-22 slide. Even their faithful fans had grown either apathetic or disgusted. Only 1,481 clicked through the Polo Grounds turnstiles to watch the final two defeats of a four-game sweep to fellow expansion team Houston in a doubleheader on September 20. They finished the season with what remains a modern major-league record 120 defeats.

The hapless bunch secured the last loss in typical fashion. Trailing the Cubs 5-1, they started an eighth-inning rally with singles by Sammy Drake and Ashburn. Joe Pignatano hit a soft liner that was caught by Chicago second baseman Ken Hubbs. Drake and Ashburn, in the wildly mistaken notion that the ball would drop, had begun running and were easily doubled and tripled off for a triple play.

No team finishes 80 games under .500 without failing in hitting, pitching, and fielding. But the Mets were not equally inept in all three. They scored enough runs to forge a far more respectable record. They placed ninth in that category ahead of Houston. But their pitching staff allowed a half-run more per game than any other team in the National League and featured three starters that lost at least 19 games in "ace" Roger Craig, Al Jackson, and Hook. Fourth starter Bob Miller sported a 1-12 mark. Even reliever Craig Anderson lost 17 of 20 decisions. But they could not be solely blamed for their struggles—led by the bungling Throneberry, the defense proved to be among the worst in major-league history. The Mets committed a disturbing 210 errors. No team in major league baseball has since compiled a higher total, though the 1963 Mets matched it.

Stengel expressed disbelief at the incompetence. He sensed the players never came together as a team. "Strangers are hard to manage," he said. "It was like spring training all year. But I expected to win more games. I was very much shocked."[5]

As for Throneberry, who personified the historical ineptitude of the 1962 Mets, he welcomed the off-season with a bit of self-effacing humor. "You think the fish will come out of the water to boo me this winter?" he asked.

Neither the fish nor the fans booed Throneberry after that season. He came to be beloved, as did the team despite maintaining its place in the National League basement. So iconic had Throneberry become that he was called upon to participate in clever Miller Lite commercials of the 1970s, well after his retirement from baseball. He would appear among the greatest athletes of their generations and ended the ads by stating simply, "I still don't know why they asked me to do this commercial."[6]

The following seasons proved scarcely better than the first for the Mets. But they did set a single-season attendance record for a last-place club as more than 900,000 streamed into the Polo Grounds to watch a team that finished an absurd 57 games out of first place. In explaining the curiously blossoming love affair, esteemed *New Yorker* writer Roger Angell opined that fans could identify more with the Mets than they could with the dominant team crosstown. "There's more Met than Yankee in all of us," he offered. "What we experience in our day-to-day lives is a lot more losing than winning, which is why we loved the Mets."[7]

And soon, they would be bungling in their new digs. Fans would besiege it to show support for their "Lovable Losers." An even stronger love affair was only a year away.

CHAPTER THREE

Oh Shea Can You See

BASEBALL HISTORIANS NEED ONLY TO PINPOINT THE HIGHLIGHT FROM the 1963 season of the Mets to understand its depths.

The date was June 23. It occurred in the fifth inning of Game 1 in a doubleheader sweep over tough Philadelphia at the Polo Grounds. A month earlier, the Mets had traded for troubled outfielder Jimmy Piersall, whose struggles with what is now known as bipolar disorder inspired the 1957 film titled *Fear Strikes Out*. Piersall slugged the first offering of the inning by Dallas Green, who later served as manager of both clubs, over the fence in right field. And rather than take the conventional jog around the bases, Piersall ran backward. He took the correct route to home but with his back to each destination.

Mets manager Stengel apparently didn't think it was funny. He cut Piersall two days later. Perhaps such clowning would have been overlooked had Piersall been tearing the cover off the ball. But his batting average had fallen under .200, and the blast that afternoon was only his second all season. Piersall had told teammates he would pull the stunt for his hundredth career home run and proved true to his word. And, as he later pointed out, he even partook in the traditional handshake with the third base coach as he began the final turn toward home plate.[1]

That the Mets had even traded for Piersall in May proved their rather muddled approach to team-building. Their status as an expansion club that was eons away from contention called desperately for a youth movement, but general manager George Weiss continued his attempt to attract fans through acquisitions that provided a blast from the past.

Included was the purchase just before the regular season of future Hall of Fame outfielder Duke Snider, who had not been a full-time starter since the Dodgers left Brooklyn for Los Angeles five years earlier. Snider performed respectably in 1963, hitting 14 home runs and even leading the woefully weak Mets attack in on-base percentage and slugging percentage. But one could argue that his at-bats should have been used as a tool for a younger prospect.

Not that the Mets completely eschewed the philosophy of everyday player development. Their 1963 lineup was sprinkled with promising talent. Included was second baseman Ron Hunt, who paced the club with a .272 batting average and 64 runs scored to finish second in the National League Rookie of the Year balloting behind none other than Pete Rose.

It had become apparent, however, that other young players, particularly offensively and defensively challenged catcher Choo-Choo Coleman, were doomed to oblivion. Rather than memories of Coleman revolving around his blossoming as a player, they will forever be centered on the comical, such as his claim of ignorance on the origin of his nickname and his reply to playing-legend-turned-broadcaster Ralph Kiner, who asked him, "What's your wife's name, and what's she like?" Answered Choo-Choo, "Her name is Mrs. Coleman, and she likes me."[2]

One might blame a sadistic schedule maker, meager Mets offense, or a combination of both for a miserable start in 1963 that nearly matched that of the year before. Forced to play rugged foes St. Louis, Milwaukee, and Cincinnati on the road to open the season, they fell to 0-8. The Mets scored just 10 runs in those games and were shut out in four of them. But they rebounded toward respectability, just as they had in 1962. Their recovery even lasted far longer. A 13-7 run capped by the first five-game winning streak in franchise history placed them on the brink of .500. They continued to bounce back from losing streaks until late June when they boasted a 29-45 record. Particularly encouraging was the pitching of Carl Willey, who had been purchased before the season from the Braves and had emerged as the ace of an improved rotation with a 2.63 earned run average. Little did anyone imagine that Willey would only win three more games for the rest of his career.

Too many passed balls played a role in a short career for Mets catcher Choo Choo Coleman.

Little did anyone imagine either that the Mets would collapse to a point where they would rival the 1962 club in futility. They indeed reverted to form with a 14-game losing streak that featured historically miserable hitting. They scored just 25 runs during that downslide and more than three only in an 11-5 shellacking by Pittsburgh. The Mets never recovered. An 11-game losing skein soon followed as they concluded the month of July with a 4-25 record. A 2-14 stretch to end the season placed their overall mark at 51-111.

Yet rather than Mets fans turning off to their team in frustration at the reality that they were making little progress toward respectability, they instead applied a more passionate embrace. More than one million fans poured into the Polo Grounds in its last season as the club ranked a strong fourth among National League teams in attendance.

Aside from competitive spirit, there seemed to be little motivation for Weiss and his front office to field a contending club, though one can claim they simply did not have the resources before the advent of free agency. Their minor-league system had yet to produce the talent necessary to win, nor did the roster boast the trade bait needed to return proven players or premier prospects.

Yet the status quo remained good enough to keep fans coming to the ballpark—73-year-old Casey Stengel stayed entrenched as manager despite strong criticism. Among those that claimed he had lost respect from his players was first baseman Jim Harkness, who leveled a strong charge after the Mets sold him to Triple-A San Diego in 1964. "Casey has been a great man for baseball as far as publicity is concerned, but the game has passed him by," Harkness claimed. "Some players he likes and some he doesn't like. The players feel it and it isn't too inspiring when the manager goes to sleep on the bench during a game."[3]

The ballyhooed opening of Shea Stadium that year proved far more inspiring—at least to the fans. A throng of 50,312 packed the new ballpark to watch the grand unveiling in game 3 of the 1964 season. True to form, the Mets continued their penchant for opening campaigns with a spate of defeats by losing to the Pirates on route to a 3-16 record. Shea opened with great fanfare. Bill Shea christened it the day before with two symbolic bottles of water, one from the Gowanus Canal near Ebbets

Field, former home of the Dodgers, and the other from the Harlem River close to the Polo Grounds. Last-minute preparations included laying new sod in the outfield during batting practice.

Bad talent had already been matched by bad luck. Carl Willey appeared destined to reach ace status after allowing no runs throughout spring training. But he broke his jaw on a vicious line drive off the bat of Detroit pinch-hitter extraordinaire Gates Brown in his final tune-up for the regular season. The blow knocked him out until June, and he was never the same. He started just two games and pitched a mere 30 innings in 1964. So fearful was Stengel to risk a potential victory that Willey was summoned only in defeats. The Mets lost all 14 games in which he appeared. Soon thereafter, arm problems struck the final blow, and Willey was out of baseball. "The whole thing was a shame because it was time for Carlton to blossom, and that finished his career," said teammate Jim Hickman years later. "Nobody realized Carl was hurt that bad because he never showed the pain. He just stood there dazed after the ball hit him."[4]

As if dazed themselves, the Mets continued on like lead character Phil Connors in the movie *Groundhog Day*. The venue had changed, but the script remained identical. Different season, same result. They were again plagued by arduously long losing streaks punctuated by offensive droughts. They averaged 1.9 runs per game during a 1-13 stretch in June while scoring more than two only twice. The limped home at 53-109.

Though Mets fans remained loyal—nearly two million filled the seats at Shea in 1964—criticism of Stengel grew. None other than the great Jackie Robinson offered that the manager was indeed snoozing during games and others questioned his managerial skills. The proud Stengel refused to succumb to the condemnation. He signed a new contract and expressed optimism headed into the 1965 season. But Father Time and fate had other ideas. He slipped and broke his wrist during spring training, then fell again in July, this time in the bathroom during a party at famed Toots Shor's restaurant while celebrating his seventy-fifth birthday. That injury and a typical 10-game losing streak current at the time of the accident were the beginning of the end for Stengel's storied managerial career. He underwent a hip implant the following day and was soon convinced by his wife to retire. He remained with the franchise only as a West Coast scout.

Replacement Wes Westrum fared no better, finishing the 1965 season at 50-112. Certainly, the most memorable events at Shea that year were not occasional Mets victories but rather the Major League All-Star Game won by the National League and the epic Beatles concert/scream-fest six weeks later.

One could hardly have imagined the Mets actually taking a step *backward*. But their roster remained plagued by has-beens and players with Triple-A talent. Even the few promising prospects were not ready to compete at the major-league level. Future contributors such as Ed Kranepool, Ron Swoboda, Bud Harrelson, and Cleon Jones were beginning to filter onto the big-league roster. But none aside from the latter ever emerged as a major offensive threat, and they certainly hadn't reached their potential heading into the latter half of the decade. The Mets also featured no premier starting pitcher to halt skids. They finished last in the National League in team earned run average behind such mediocrities as Jack Fisher and Al Jackson, as well as 43-year-old southpaw Warren Spahn, who was making his second-to-last stop before ending a Hall-of-Fame career.

Weiss tried to force square pegs into round holes, mostly due to a lack of development and production from the farm system. There were occasional exceptions, such as Jerry Grote, who arrived in 1966 to finally solidify the troubled catching position for a decade. Grote boasted little power, but he hit for a decent average in a pitching-dominated era and worked well with the staff.

Rather than force-feeding young position players and starters into the rotation, Weiss continued to trade for veterans who could at least fill holes temporarily. Among them was third baseman Ken Boyer, who two years earlier had earned National League Most Valuable Player honors with St. Louis. Boyer, who arrived as part of a deal that sent Jackson to the Cardinals, led a bad-but-balanced attack in 1966 with a mere 61 runs batted in and was sent to the Chicago White Sox the following July. Meanwhile, pitchers who arrived via trade such as Dennis Ribant, Bob Friend, and Bob Shaw were either one-season stopgaps who faded fast or former standouts at the end of the baseball trail.

Cleon Jones batted .340 to help the Mets snag the National League crown in 1969.

The woeful absence of young talent, particularly in the major-league rotation, precluded any optimism of a quick turnaround. Poor drafting didn't help. The Mets blundered badly in the 1966 amateur draft by selecting high school catcher Steve Chilcott (who never reached the majors) first overall rather than Arizona State stud outfielder Reggie Jackson, who would blossom into one of the most prodigious sluggers and clutch hitters in baseball history.

They did, however, show a bit of a spark that year, hanging around the periphery of mediocrity for most of the season. Despite their inevitable early fade from the pennant race—they were nine games out by May 13—they avoided the long losing streaks that had destroyed previous Mets editions. They dropped no more than five straight at any point through July 4 and rebounded from a seven-game skein later that month to win a franchise-best seven straight games, including successive doubleheader sweeps of Houston. The 35-year-old Friend even dipped into the fountain of youth to conclude the winning stretch with a 3-0 defeat of the eventual National League champion Dodgers. The Mets finished the month on a 12-4 roll and a very uncharacteristic eight games under .500. They were even within shouting distance of sixth place.

Optimism was soon replaced by reality. The Mets dropped 40 of their last 59 games. Included in the collapse was a 5-20 stretch. But they finished out of the cellar and avoided 100 defeats for the first time in franchise history. So appreciative of the effort was Westrum that he provided champagne to his players following a year-ending loss to Houston.

Westrum could have saved some of the bubbly for a going-away party for the 72-year-old Weiss, who retired during the off-season. He was replaced by Vaughan "Bing" Devine, who had been serving as his assistant for two years after building the Cardinals into a World Series champion earlier in the decade as general manager through the acquisition of African-American talent such as Bob Gibson, Lou Brock, Bill White, and Curt Flood. Devine, who had won *Sporting News* Executive of the Year honors in 1963 and 1964, served in that capacity with the Mets only for one season. But by that time, he had engineered one astute move that would bring the greatest pitcher in franchise history and among the finest ever in major league baseball to the mound at Shea Stadium.

CHAPTER FOUR

Tom Terrific

IT HAS BEEN STATED RATHER MYSTICALLY THAT LUCK DOES NOT EXIST on its own. Those who believe that as a truth claim people make their own luck. They feel it is a product of hard work. The opposite philosophy is that it's better to be lucky than good—especially in sports.

Whatever the reality, the Mets got darn lucky twice in 1966. Their first bit of good fortune was realized when Major League Baseball commissioner William Eckart voided what he deemed to be Tom Seaver's illegal deal with the Atlanta Braves. The University of Southern California right-hander had already been assigned to Triple-A Richmond, but the team had broken major league rules that state no organization can sign a college player while his season is already in progress. He had yet to pitch for USC in 1966, but the team had begun play when he signed with the Braves. So Seaver, who was to be the prize jewel of the Atlanta organization, remained unattached. He was made available to any team willing to match the contract.

Mets general manager George Weiss, who would retire after the season, balked at that prospect. But assistant Bing Devine wanted the Mets to pursue the talented Seaver, who would cost them the rather hefty sum at the time of $50,000. "(Weiss) didn't know anything about him," Devine said. "I made a big case, and I recall it was only before we had to make a decision and agree to that, and [he] finally shook his head, I'm sure not wanted to do it, and said, 'If you people make such a big case of it, go ahead.'"[1]

It was the most important nod in franchise history. Desperate for a rotation ace or even a viable starting pitcher, the Mets joined Cleveland and Philadelphia in a drawing to land Seaver. And Lady Luck smiled upon the New Yorkers. The Mets won the contest and assigned him to Triple-A Jacksonville. Despite his status as a minor leaguer, Seaver was already the best pitcher in the organization, even given an influx of mound talent such as blossoming Jerry Koosman and flame-throwing Nolan Ryan.

He had certainly been working at it for a while. His love affair with baseball was already pronounced as a three-year-old when he played pretend games with imaginary friends George and Charlie in the backyard of his home in Fresno, California. The little Seaver would jump around and run the bases as his mother watched out the window. His competitive nature reflected that of his father, a tremendous golfer who, in 1930, nearly reached the final round of the US Amateur championship and two years later won a tournament at Stanford University, where he also played football and basketball.

The elder Seaver, who worked with a company that harvested and shipped raisins around the country, passed on his athletic prowess to his kids. Katie excelled in volleyball and swimming at Stanford, Charles swam on the University of California varsity, and Carol majored in physical education at UCLA. Apparently not wishing to leave any major California college out as Seaver contributors, Tom signed on to play at USC. The youngest of the four spoke about the competitive spirit that emerged as a Seaver trait.

"Our family was always competitive," Seaver said. "Even when my father was working around the house he wanted perfection, and he tried to instill that striving in us, too. I learned a real respect for the value of work, not as a means—not just for the money it can bring you—but for the pleasure of doing something as well as you can, as near perfectly as you can. I wish today that I could use the same amount of concentration on other things that I put into pitching, but if I could, I would not enjoy baseball as much as I do. The thing I appreciate about the game is that it is one of the few places left where a person like myself can show his individuality."[2]

Long before his college career, Seaver had established a style on the mound that maximized both body and mind. He earned a reputation at Fresno High School as a pitcher who did not require strikeouts to succeed. "Tom was a thinking pitcher," said Dick Selma, a fellow Fresno High alum and future teammate. "He knew how to set up a hitter by working the corners of the plate and the batter would usually pop the ball . . . for an easy out."[3]

The easy outs continued at Fresno City College, where Seaver embarked on a personal 11-game winning streak and shattered one school strikeout record after another to pique the interest of scouts. He proved his worthiness of a Division I scholarship by pitching for the semipro Goldpanners in Alaska, then joined the Trojans as a junior in 1965 and compiled a 10-2 record while fanning 100 in 100 innings.

Seaver wasted no time in his meteoric rise to The Show. He tossed four shutouts for Jacksonville, inspiring manager Solly Hemus to praise him for his maturity as a pitcher and readiness for the big leagues. Legendary Orioles manager Earl Weaver, who was guiding the Rochester club at the time, lauded Seaver for the pinpoint control of his fastball and slider and urged Baltimore general manager Harry Dalton to consider trading for him. The Orioles were loaded with talent—they had embarked in 1966 on a World Series championship run—but one could not have imagined the pitching-poor Mets dispatching Seaver anywhere.

Devine overhauled the roster heading into the 1967 season. Most shocking was a trade that sent versatile Jim Hickman and second baseman Ron Hunt to the Dodgers for slugging outfielder Tommy Davis in an attempt to add power. But though Davis remained productive, batting .302 and leading the team in home runs and runs batted in, it had become apparent he would never again match or even approach the production from his epic 1962 season when he led the National League with a .346 average and 153 RBI. Davis lasted just one season in the Big Apple before he was sent to the White Sox in a wise swap that landed outfield standout Tommie Agee, who brought a combination of speed and power previously unseen in the Mets lineup.

The 1967 Mets never generated a strong sense of optimism. They fell 7½ games behind first-place Cincinnati by the end of April and

Tom Seaver about to show off the wicked stuff that placed him among the greatest pitchers in baseball history.

Ripped off from the White Sox in a steal of a deal, Tommie Agee provided punch to a previously punchless Mets offense.

continued to fade. A decent run in July was followed by a 3-14 stretch. A 5-22 slide in August and September doomed the club to another 100-loss season, its fifth in six years since expanding into existence. The Mets finished last in the National League in runs scored and a lowly eighth in team earned run average.

But there was one glimmer of hope—the rookie who pitched half of the team's 36 complete games in 1967. Seaver performed brilliantly in showing the poise and control that would remain trademarks throughout his Hall of Fame career. He allowed no more than four earned runs in any of his first 14 starts, struggled in some outings in July and August, including a second-inning knockout in Houston, then finished with a flourish, winning four consecutive decisions in September. Seaver not only ended the season with a 16-13 record and three more wins than any Mets pitcher in six years, but he earned a save in a 2-1 National League victory in the All-Star Game. It came as no surprise when he became the first Rookie of the Year from a last-place team. "This is a bigger thrill to me than being named to the All-Star team," he said after receiving the honor. "You only get one chance to be Rookie of the Year. If you're good you can make the All-Star team several times in your career."[4]

Little could Seaver have realized that he would earn 10 All-Star Game nods in a Mets uniform. A team so desperate for an ace finally had one. And he arrived in the big leagues at the right time—during the most dominant pitching era in baseball history. Seaver fit right into the Year of the Pitcher in 1968, teamed with blossoming Jerry Koosman to form a dynamite one-two punch at the head of a deep and talented rotation. Only an outrageous season from Cardinals ace Bob Gibson prevented Seaver and Koosman from competing for the 1968 Cy Young Award.

Seaver had not only emerged as a stud, but his greatness also signaled the start of a successful shift in attitude and confidence within the organization. A drive to win had shifted into high gear and accelerated. The Mets were no world-beaters by any stretch of the imagination, but their 73-89 record proved far superior to any they had previously posted. And their 2.72 team ERA in 1968 ranked a fine fourth in the National League. It was heady stuff for the suddenly not-as-woebegone club.

Southpaw Jerry Koosman played a key role in elevating the Mets from patsies to champions.

"Now, for the first time, we know when we go out and play that youth is taking over and we have pitchers who can hold the other guy off," said outfielder Ron Swoboda in a *Sports Illustrated* article published in May. "It isn't like other years when a lot of guys were just putting in their time and adding to their pension plans—get it over and let's get the paycheck. Seaver showed a lot of people that a young guy could win with the Mets because he thought everything over so well and you could tell that losing tore him up. It went down the line to the rest of the young guys, like myself."[5]

Seaver maintained his brilliance beyond the Miracle Mets season of 1969. He proved himself the most consistently dominant pitcher in the National League and arguably in the sport over the next five years. He led the NL in earned run average three times from 1970 to 1973 and six times in strikeouts through 1976. His combination of control within the strike zone and pure stuff resulted in averages of one strikeout per inning in 1970 and 1971, a mean feat for pitchers of that generation. The result was three Cy Young Awards and a lock as a Hall of Famer a decade before retirement.

Yet despite an intense focus on his craft that allowed him to affirm his greatness every season, Seaver proved unafraid to react to changing times both outside and inside the sports arena during the turbulent sixties and well beyond. His feelings about the American involvement in the Vietnam War, which had reached its peak, were revealed to the nation during the 1969 World Series when he was quoted in the *New York Times*. "If the Mets can win the World Series, then we can get out of Vietnam," he said. "I think it's perfectly ridiculous what we're doing about the Vietnam situation. It's absurd."[6]

Also absurd in Seaver's mind was the reserve clause that had tied players to their teams in perpetuity. Seaver, who served as the Mets' union representative as Marvin Miller and the players finally gained their freedom, followed with interest the journeys of fellow mound standouts Andy Messersmith and Dave McNally, who played the entire 1975 seasons without contracts and were soon thereafter declared free agents.

The shackles had been broken. Seaver had fought successfully with his compatriots to create a fair negotiating environment. Now he yearned to reap the benefits. He had rebounded from a rare mediocre season in 1974 in which he compiled an 11-11 record to double that victory total in 1975 and earn his third Cy Young Award. He demanded a three-year, $825,000 deal, motivating team president M. Donald Grant to threaten to trade him to the Dodgers for veteran standout starter Don Sutton.

Seaver remained in the catbird seat. Upon tossing his first pitch in the 1976 season, he would become a "10-and-5" pitcher. Under the new rules, any player with 10 years in the big leagues and five with the same team could reject any trade. Grant needed to send him packing before then to close a deal but understood the public relations nightmare involved in unloading Seaver. So he caved, offering his all-star right-hander a three-year contract with an annual base salary of $225,000. Though Seaver signed, his professional relationship with Grant had been ruined.

The end of that marriage was near. Seaver grew further disenchanted by the refusal of the organization to dip into the growing free-agent pool and address a lack of hitting that had remained a problem since the birth of the franchise—even the 1969 Miracle Mets only finished ninth among 12 National League teams in runs scored. Poor run support reared its ugly head again in 1976 as his teammates tallied a mere 14 runs in his 11 defeats. Seaver lost all four of his decisions during a six-week stretch in the second half of the season despite posting a sparkling 2.13 ERA. Seaver became outspoken in his criticism of the club and wondered aloud if he should have opted for free agency rather than signing with the Mets in 1976, prompting Grant to call him an "ingrate" and state that he would "try to run our business in a sensible way."[7]

Most in the media backed Seaver in his battle with Grant. Not among them was aging *Daily News* legend Dick Young, whose old-school beliefs about new-school labor relations in baseball resulted in a clash with Seaver. Young labeled the Mets ace a "troublemaker" that no other team would be willing to sign. Seaver did his talking on the field in early 1977 with a 4-0 record and a fifth one-hitter (two of which ended with two out in the ninth). Yet Young continued writing with a poison pen, offering that Seaver was a "pouting, griping, morale-breaking clubhouse lawyer."[8]

The die was not yet cast. Seaver had the upper hand as a 10/5 player. He was performing so well on the mound that general manager Joe McDonald, who had been negotiating a trade with Cincinnati with Seaver as the centerpiece, offered to extend his contract three years at $1.1 million. Seaver agreed in principle to the deal until Young wrote a piece claiming that the hurler had been angered when Nolan Ryan, who had long since left for the Angels, signed a more lucrative contract than what McDonald had offered. Seaver had become fed up with Young and Grant. He fumed to public relations director Arthur Richman that he wanted out and had reversed course on inking the extension. Seaver would welcome a trade to Cincinnati.

And that is what he got. The Mets sent him to the Reds for pitcher Pat Zachry, infielder Doug Flynn, and outfielders Steve Henderson and Dan Norman in a trade forever known as the Midnight Massacre. Zachry faded after one strong season. Flynn performed well afield but managed little production at the plate. Only Henderson, who placed second in the 1977 Rookie of the Year voting, brought a decent return. Meanwhile, Seaver became the personification of Ol' Man River, pitching 10 more years and winning 129 more games, including 16 with the White Sox at age 40. One of those seasons was a for old-times-sake reuniting with the Mets in 1983 in which he posted a 9-14 mark and likely felt a sense of déjà vu as his offense failed to score for him.

Seaver finally retired in 1986, ironically the same year the Mets captured their only other World Series crown. The first-ballot Hall of Famer will forever be remembered after his death in September 2020, not only as the greatest pitcher in franchise history but also as among the best to ever grace a major-league uniform.

CHAPTER FIVE

From Chumps to Champs

THE MIRACLE OF THE MIRACLE METS DID NOT TAKE FORM WHEN THEY arrived for spring training. The seeds were planted nearly 15 months earlier.

It was November 27, 1967. Passionate fans might not have had an appetite for the Thanksgiving dinner to come had they thought about their woebegone team, which had lost 101 games under manager Wes Westrum and interim replacement Salty Parker. Despite the emergence of ace Tom Seaver, the franchise gave no indication of a breakthrough. But on that day, they completed a unique trade that would set their course for an upward trajectory. Vice-president George Murphy, who a month later was named general manager when Bing Devine accepted the same job with the Cardinals, sent nondescript pitcher Bill Denehy and $100,000 to the Senators for manager Gil Hodges.

Three factors weighed in the Mets' favor despite the reality that Washington had no intention of letting Hodges go. Murphy was an old friend and roommate of Senators GM George Selkirk. Mets board chairman M. Donald Grant insisted Murphy do all in his power to secure the services of the former Met. And the Senators needed the money. They had placed among the bottom three in American League attendance every season since 1961, when a new franchise took over for the one that left to become the Minnesota Twins.

Hodges had not engineered any miracles in the nation's capital, but he had improved the club in each of his five seasons as manager. He guided the 1967 team to a surprising 76-85 record and sixth-place finish.

And he continued to make lemonade out of lemons with a 1968 Mets bunch woefully lacking in hitting. He managed them to a 73-89 record, their best to date, while applying an effectively innovative approach.

Among his first moves was to hire former major-league catcher and minor-league manager Rube Walker as pitching coach. Hodges understood the qualifications of a catcher to maximize the vast promise of his moundsmen. Hodges also added former catchers Joe Pignatano and Yogi Berra to his staff. The new skipper was merely playing to his strengths. The Mets boasted tremendous pitching potential in Seaver, soon-to-be National League Rookie of the Year Jerry Koosman, young Gary Gentry, and 22-year-old fireballer Nolan Ryan. As the Year of the Pitcher approached and with an attack in place that would average fewer than three runs per game, Hodges knew he had to ride his arms to victory.

Walker not only instituted a five-man rotation that has become the norm in major league baseball, but he also thrived stressing both the physical and mental aspects of pitching. He installed regimens in which his hurlers ran hard to stay in shape and limited throwing between starts. He taught his pitchers how to identify issues in their deliveries and pitch to their strengths. Among his projects was encouraging Koosman to drop his slider in exchange for a more effective curveball. Soon the young pitchers were throwing like veterans. "We loved him. Rube was like my father," said Koosman.[1]

Hodges also pioneered a platoon system that gained popularity in decades to follow. One could debate its effectiveness in 1968 and beyond, given the pronounced lack of hitting ability on the roster beyond Cleon Jones and Tommie Agee—even they faded in the early 1970s. But Hodges believed platooning based on right-handed or left-handed mound opponents would maximize the little talent available and produce in all his players a sense of involvement. Seventeen Mets received at least 119 plate appearances in 1968.

The approach worked well enough to at least vault the Mets into the realm of mediocrity through the first half of the season. They scored enough runs to forge a 38-42 record in early July. But they did not exceed five runs in any game thereafter for the next month and averaged just 2.6 per game in September to fade into ninth place. The rotation proved so powerful that the Mets even won four during a 10-game stretch in which just 14 runners crossed the plate.

The late collapse punctuated by a mild heart attack suffered by the 44-year-old Hodges in late September provided little hope that the Mets could finally shed their well-earned reputation as National League punching bag. Neither did their acquisition inactivity in the off-season. One could only hope that enough of their hitters would exceed expectations in providing support for a brilliant young pitching staff.

The impact of Hodges proved all-encompassing. He defined the roles of every player heading into the 1969 season. He altered their mental and emotional states. His emphasis on fundamentals gave them confidence. "He was so upbeat it changed the culture of the team," offered shortstop Bud Harrelson. "Because of Hodges' optimism, instead of being chronic and laughable losers . . . we began to think of ourselves as winners . . . when we started to win it was because of him."[2]

Hodges left no stone unturned trying to improve his team. He used relationships with former Brooklyn and Los Angeles Dodgers teammates to impart wisdom during spring training and throughout the regular season. Among them was legendary left-hander Sandy Koufax, who taught Koosman how to change speeds on his curveball.

The downfall in 1968 showed that teaching confidence could not translate to success overnight. It did not turn duds into studs early the following year either. The 1969 Mets provided the expansion Montreal Expos with their first-ever victory on Opening Day, then lost five of six to the sizzling Chicago Cubs to fall to 9-14 and into fifth place in a six-team division, a whopping eight games out of first. The Mets simply boasted too much pitching to sink into oblivion, though a five-game losing streak in which they were outscored 36-9 dropped their record to 18-23.

They could have hit rock bottom against lowly San Diego on May 28. Koosman struck out 15, which would remain a career-high (he tied it in 1980), and pitched shutout ball for 10 innings. But the game remained scoreless until Harrelson singled for the winning run in the eleventh. The harrowing triumph seemed to propel the Mets into the stratosphere. They won 11 straight games—including sweeps of former New York residents Dodgers and Giants—to soar into second place, where they remained aside from one day until their final push to the pennant.

The defeat of the Padres also marked the coronation of a heretofore struggling left-hander named Tug McGraw as one of the finest closers in Mets history. He had scuffled mightily as a starting pitcher upon his arrival in the big leagues four years earlier, even spending the entire 1968 season at Triple-A Jacksonville. McGraw was mashed in three consecutive starts earlier that month before throwing a shutout inning to earn the win against San Diego. He gained his first save three days later in a victory over San Francisco with four strikeouts in two clean innings and was on his way. Hodges soon made the fateful decision to keep him in the bullpen. The screwball specialist became unhittable, allowing just two earned runs in 38 innings over the last nine weeks of the regular season.

"The only other pitcher with a screwball was Jim Brewer of the Dodgers, so the hitters weren't used to seeing it," McGraw said. "By June, I was still pitching well and Gil called me into his office. He said, 'Tug, I have three pieces of advice for you. One, I think you should think about staying in the bullpen permanently. You could be a great reliever and at best an average starter. Two, this team needs a late-inning stopper, and I want you to be my stopper. Three, I think you'll make a lot more money as a reliever than as a starter. Now it's up to you.' I said, 'Gil, if you think that's the way for me to go, I'm there already.' The rest is history."[3]

The final piece of the personnel puzzle was put into place on June 15, the day after a loss to the Cubs pushed the Mets six games off the lead. That is when they acquired veteran first baseman Donn Clendenon from Montreal for four players, including promising pitcher Steve Renko, who would emerge as a rotation standout for the Expos. Clendenon, who had thrived as a power hitter with Pittsburgh until joining Montreal via the expansion draft, lost playing time but gained a pennant race with the Mets. He fit ideally into the Hodges platoon system as a badly needed run producer. Clendenon hit 12 home runs and drove in 37 in just 202 at-bats following the trade.

The acquisition did not transform the club into a steamroller. They became a machine instead that accelerated and stopped while the Cubs continued to win. The Mets won eight of 10 after the trade, then lost

Screwball specialist Tug McGraw emerged as one of the finest closers of all-time.

four in a row. They won 14 of 19 in late June and early July, then again dropped four straight games. They fell into third place and 10 games behind Chicago on August 13 after a sweep in Houston. The Mets appeared destined for their first above-.500 finish but doomed to watch the playoffs and World Series on television with the rest of America.

Then they got hot. White-hot. They allowed three earned runs over 59 innings during a six-game winning streak that included three shutouts at the expense of San Diego and San Francisco. The bats then came to life in another six-game tear that victimized the Dodgers and Padres. Meanwhile, the Cubs began to lose. They were hearing footsteps. An 8-11 stretch in August shrunk their lead to a mere 2½ games.

A five-game winning streak that extended into September stretched their advantage back to five and appeared to have staved off the Mets. But the tidal waves heading in opposite directions had merely slowed. They could not be halted. Chicago was in the midst of an eight-game losing streak when they arrived at Shea Stadium for what could have been a make-or-break two-game series on September 8 in which the Mets had Koosman and Seaver lined up to pitch. The former had struggled in his previous two starts but took advantage of a two-run homer by Agee and completed a 3-2 victory with 13 strikeouts. The deficit had dropped to 1½ games.

Then even Lady Luck donned a Mets uniform the next night as the two clubs sent their aces to the mound—Seaver and Ferguson Jenkins. She sent a black cat to scurry in front of the Cubs dugout in the fourth inning. The feline cast a glance at manager Leo Durocher before toddling off. Though Shea was often frequented by stray cats, Chicago was already down 4-0 and scored its only run of the game immediately after the cat departed, and few at the time gave it much thought, but the incident became part of baseball folklore. Legend prevailed, and the black cat had doomed the Cubs.

Reality, of course, screams out that luck had nothing to do with it. The Mets had simply emerged as the premier team in the National League. They crisscrossed the Cubs in the standings at a full sprint. They won 10 straight while Chicago lost 11 of 12, and it was over. New York had long since claimed the National League East crown when it rubbed salt in the wound by winning the opener of a two-game series at Wrigley Field to end the regular season. A sellout throng of 54,928 had watched them clinch the most unlikely title in baseball history with a 6-0 Gentry shutout of St. Louis a week earlier. The Amazin' Mets had amazingly gone from five games down to nine games up in one month.

Their work was far from done. The 1969 season marked the first of division play in major league baseball. The Mets needed to defeat Western Division champion Atlanta to earn a World Series berth. No sweat. Their rotation was on an outrageous roll. Mets pitching had allowed just 12 runs during a nine-game winning streak that extended to October 1. Included were four consecutive shutouts—two by Gentry. And Seaver seemed unhittable. He was an incredible 12-5 in 1969 when his team scored three runs or less, a winning percentage of .706 that remains the best in baseball since the live-ball era began in 1920. So durable was Seaver that he had not allowed an earned run in the 18 ninth innings in which he had pitched, tying a major-league record that, given the lack of complete games in the modern era, will likely never be broken.

The Braves simply could not match up on the mound. But, remarkably, the super staff did not dominate the series. Rather, it was the offense that burned Atlanta. The Mets scored 27 runs in a three-game blitz that catapulted them into a showdown with powerful Baltimore for all the marbles. And though premier hitters Jones and Agee performed well and combined for three home runs in the series, they had plenty of company as lesser-lights Art Shamsky, Wayne Garrett, and Ken Boswell all slugged the Braves into oblivion.

The Orioles promised far tougher competition. They were considered among the greatest clubs in baseball history. They had blown away the American League with 109 wins and a sweep of Minnesota in the division series. They could match the Mets on the mound with ace Jim Palmer and 20-game-winners Mike Cuellar and Dave McNally. And they boasted a far more potent batting attack that featured Hall of Famers Frank Robinson and Brooks Robinson, as well as burly home-run slugger Boog Powell. Even their fielding ranked atop the junior circuit. The Braves were pushovers in comparison.

Hodges yearned to ensure that his players realized the Orioles also put on their pants one leg at a time. He called a clubhouse meeting before the series and provided a simple message. "You guys don't have to be anything but what you've been," he said.[4]

Seaver was not what he had been in Game 1. Though he was on six days rest, he admitted to being tired. After all, he and Koosman had started 24 of the last 56 games of the regular season as Hodges discarded his strict adherence to the five-man rotation to clinch a playoff spot. Seaver struggled with his curve, and the Birds took advantage, knocking him out after five innings in a 4-1 victory that had some believing they were simply too strong for the upstart Mets.

The opposite proved true. The Mets had not won 41 of their last 53 games as a potential patsy in the World Series. They staged a two-out rally in the ninth to win Game 2 behind a brilliant performance from Koosman in which he maintained a no-hitter through the sixth inning.

A crowd of 56,335 packed Shea Stadium two days later to witness Game 3, otherwise known as "The Tommie Agee Show." The Mets centerfielder and leadoff hitter hogged the spotlight from beginning to end. He opened the bottom of the first with a home run to center field off the great Palmer, then stole a two-run double from Elrod Hendricks with a backhanded grab on a dead sprint in the fourth. Agee saved his best for last, racing into right-center to make a diving grab of a Paul Blair liner with the bases loaded in the seventh. "I held my breath for a minute," said Ryan, who had entered that inning to preserve the shutout begun by Gentry. "But then I saw [Agee] tap his glove and I knew it was all right. Every time he does that, I know he's going to catch it."[5]

Agee had saved five runs in a 5-0 victory and both impressed and depressed legendary Orioles manager Earl Weaver. "We had one run in the last 18 innings and Agee had five today," he lamented. "If they had to play without him, we'd have won."[6]

Seaver required no crystal ball to predict the series would not return to Baltimore. He and Koosman were lined up to start the next two at Shea. And Seaver was not about to allow the Birds to fly again. Thanks to a Clendenon home run, he took a 1-0 lead into the ninth inning in Game 4 before allowing two singles. Hodges strolled to the mound. "How do you feel?" he asked Seaver. "I'm running out of gas, but I still have a few pitches left," came the reply. Other managers might have removed any starter who admitted he was running on fumes. But not Hodges. And not with Seaver. The manager refused to remove his ace.

Mets fans wished he had when Brooks Robinson slammed a line drive to right that seemed destined to find green. But right fielder Ron Swoboda, who risked allowing the tying and go-ahead runs to score by leaving his feet, made a sprawling grab. The result was a sacrifice fly that tied the game. Seaver escaped yet another jam in the tenth on his 150th pitch of the game, a total in the modern era that would get a manager fired, then he watched his teammates score the game-winner on a Jerry Grote double and rare Baltimore error.

The die was cast. The Mets were a team of destiny. The Orioles were beaten, even after McNally and Frank Robinson slammed third-inning home runs off Koosman the next day to give them a 3-0 lead. Jones reached base to lead off the sixth when Hodges showed shoe polish on a ball he claimed had skipped into the dugout after hitting the batter in the foot. Whether that was the actual ball McNally had thrown remains clouded in mystery, but it gave the Mets a bit of impetus when Clendenon sewed up World Series Most Valuable Player honors by slamming a hanging curve for a two-run homer, and light-hitting second baseman Al Weis tied the game at 3-3 with a solo smash. After Koosman retired 15 of 16 batters from the third inning forward, doubles by Jones and Swoboda gave the Mets the only run they would need to clinch arguably the most improbable championship in American sports history.

While delirious fans rushed the field, the Mets came together at the mound to celebrate, then retreated to their clubhouse to douse one another in champagne. Most had experienced the misery of daily defeat in seasons past in that same locker room. As the witty Swoboda so perceptively stated, the achievement of his team "will give heart to every loser in America."[7]

Little doubt remained in the minds of those whooping it up who made it all possible. It was Hodges. Veteran New York baseball writer Wayne Coffey spoke of the universal respect the manager had earned from his charges. "Every single player told me, in so many words, that the '69 Mets would not have won the Series, or even close to it, without Gil Hodges," Coffey said.[8]

Even God called it a miracle—or at least the Lord as portrayed by venerable actor and comedian George Burns in the 1977 comedy hit *Oh, God!* in which the character claimed the following about his rare performing of miracles: "The last miracle I did was the 1969 Mets. Before that, I think you have to go back to the Red Sea."[9]

Soon the streets were filled with a million adoring fans for a ticker-tape parade. The throngs that once embraced the Mets as lovable losers were now hailing them as champions. Now they were the Even More Amazin' Mets.

CHAPTER SIX

Yogi and the Years of Mediocrity

THERE WAS NO ELEPHANT IN THE ROOM IN THE HEARTS AND MINDS OF the Mets or their fans as the turbulent sixties ended. One and all were too happy celebrating a shocking World Series champion to worry about what continued as an on-field problem even in 1969. And that was a lack of hitting. The platoon system expertly and effectively employed by manager Gil Hodges had maximized their limited offensive potential, but the Mets still ranked ninth out of 12 National League clubs in runs scored.

The untimely passing of general manager Johnny Murphy from a heart attack in January could have complicated matters, but replacement Bob Scheffing provided a smooth transition after having served as director of player development. Among the last Murphy moves, one proved to be perhaps his worst. He traded outfield prospect Amos Otis to Kansas City for third baseman Joe Foy, who had peaked in 1969 and struggled both at the plate and in the field upon joining the Mets. Otis blossomed into a five-tool standout and one of the greatest all-around players in Royals history.

Scheffing followed two years later by misreading the potential of a hitting prospect that could have beefed up a weak lineup for more than a decade. After being used sparingly by Hodges in 1970 and 1971, outfielder Ken Singleton was dispatched to Montreal along with shortstop Tim Foli and first baseman Mike Jorgensen for slugger Rusty Staub. Expos fans condemned the trading of "Le Grande Orange," who had been their favorite player since the birth of the franchise in 1969. But Singleton emerged as a Most Valuable Player candidate with Montreal and Baltimore. Meanwhile, Foli provided stability at shortstop for five seasons, and Jorgensen did the same at first.

Staub did not disappoint but certainly proved unworthy of that haul. A broken hand sustained on a hit by pitch courtesy of Cincinnati southpaw Ross Grimsley wiped out the second half of his 1972 season. Staub not only graced the city with his philanthropy and even his culinary artistry as a world-class chef, but he also performed well offensively for the Mets over the next three seasons. He enjoyed arguably the finest year in franchise history to that point in 1975 by batting .282 with 19 home runs and 105 runs batted in. But Scheffing compounded the ill-fated deal that brought Staub to New York by engineering a trade that sent him packing to Detroit for all-but-cooked 35-year-old left-hander Mickey Lolich. Owner Lorinda de Roulet nixed a proposed trade with Baltimore that had been approved by minority owner M. Donald Grant and would have brought in promising third baseman Doug DeCinces, who had a long and fruitful career. Roulet, who had assumed ownership of the team upon the passing of her mother, Joan Payson, rejected the idea of receiving a rookie for Staub. The slugger then averaged 106 RBI over the next three years for the Tigers and drove in a career-high 121 in 1978.

The result of the wheeling and dealing was offensive doldrums that prevented the Mets from taking advantage of a premier pitching staff that still featured Tom Seaver, Jerry Koosman, and closer Tug McGraw, as well as emerging right-hander Jon Matlack, who exploded onto the scene in 1972 to compile a 15-10 record and a brilliant 2.32 earned run average, and win NL Rookie of the Year honors.

The team gained little consistency from its hitters in the early 1970s. Heroes of 1969, such as Tommie Agee, Cleon Jones, Donn Clendenon, and Art Shamsky, all produced well in 1970, but the latter two faded badly the following year, and all four had lost their mojo by 1972. The Mets continued in vain piecemealing a viable offense. They ranked in the bottom half of the National League in runs scored every season throughout the decade, placing dead last in 1977 and 1978. By that time, a team that drew more fans than any other in the NL every year from 1970 to 1972 ranked last in attendance. Potential patrons decided they would

Rusty Staub arrived from Montreal to strengthen the lineup in the early 1970s.

rather stay home than watch a club that had not only transgressed from mediocre to lousy but was boring as well.

One shocking moment in time did not, in hindsight, significantly alter the course of Mets fortunes on the field, but it proved tragic nevertheless. The date was April 2, 1972. A players strike had, for the first time, wiped out part of a season, but a settlement had assured that games would begin five days later. The 47-year-old Hodges had just completed a round of golf with his coaches in Palm Beach when he fell to the pavement in cardiac arrest. He died that evening.

The stunning event devastated those who knew him. Hodges was revered more as a person than a player and manager. Among those shattered upon hearing the news was former Dodgers teammate and Hall of Fame pitcher Don Drysdale. "Gil's death absolutely shattered me," he said. "I just flew apart. I didn't leave my apartment in Texas for three days. I didn't want to see anybody. I couldn't get myself to go to the funeral. It was like I'd lost part of my family."[1]

Taking over for Hodges, Yogi Berra displayed a different managerial style despite having coached under Hodges for four years. He proved far less a disciplinarian than his predecessor, trusting his players to stay in shape and take their work seriously. Berra also rejected the platoon system embraced by Hodges, preferring instead to provide those he considered his best hitters full-time status. It did not matter—neither manager boasted enough productive batters to transform the Mets into a strong offensive club.

The Berra tactics appeared to be reaping benefits through June 1, 1970. The Mets had already concluded winning streaks of seven and 11 games and owned a 30-11 record, five games ahead of the pack in the NL East. Staub was sizzling at the plate. Also hot were Jones, Agee, and veteran third baseman Jim Fregosi, who had been acquired in an historically ill-fated off-season trade that shipped future Hall of Fame hurler Nolan Ryan to the California Angels. The house of cards began to fall when a broken hand sidelined Staub. The offense quickly dried up. The Mets amazingly failed to score more than four runs in any of their first 21 games in July, a stretch in which they fell from a tie for first place to seven games out.

LAWRENCE PETER BERRA
"YOGI"
NEW YORK, A.L. 1946 - 1963
NEW YORK, N.L. 1965
PLAYED ON MORE PENNANT-WINNERS (14) AND
WORLD CHAMPIONS (10) THAN ANY PLAYER IN
HISTORY. HAD 358 HOME RUNS AND LIFETIME
.285 BATTING AVERAGE. SET MANY RECORDS
FOR CATCHERS, INCLUDING 148 CONSECUTIVE
GAMES WITHOUT AN ERROR. VOTED A.L. MOST
VALUABLE PLAYER 1951 - 54 - 55. MANAGED
YANKEES TO PENNANT IN 1964.

Yogi Berra managed the Mets to the pennant in 1973, nine years after guiding the Yankees to the American League crown.

Not even the return to the Big Apple of 41-year-old legend Willie Mays, whom the Mets acquired in mid-May from San Francisco in a sentimentally driven deal, could stop the slide. The "Say Hey Kid" still had a bit of pop left in his bat but was a shadow of his former self at the plate and in center. His presence took away at-bats from Agee, who lost 54 points on his batting average after the Mays acquisition.

A heist engineered by Scheffing that November did not result in more victories in 1973, but certainly allowed the Mets to remain competitive in a woefully weak division. The general manager sent fading starting pitcher Gary Gentry and nondescript reliever Danny Frisella to Atlanta for left-hander George Stone and all-star second baseman Felix Millan. Stone performed so well out of the bullpen that Berra placed him in the rotation, where he thrived down the stretch. But it was Millan that made the deal a steal. While Frisella proved mediocre with the Braves and arm problems were spelling the end of Gentry's once-promising career, Millan led the 1973 Mets in batting average at .290 and in runs scored with 82. And he continued to perform well for New York until retiring after the 1977 season.

Not that the trade sent the Mets skyrocketing. Rather, the club seemed to have plummeted hopelessly out of the race by early June. A continued free fall motivated calls for Berra to be fired. One assumed his team was doomed in early August with a 48-60 record that rested them 11½ games behind first-place St. Louis. Catching the Cardinals, let alone catapulting every other team in the division, seemed impossible.

The spotlight had shifted to heretofore brilliant closer McGraw. The iconoclastic reliever who threw the screwball on the mound and was known as a screwball off it (he earned the nickname "Tug" as a baby for his aggressiveness in breastfeeding) had collapsed in the first half of the year. A blown save on July 7 against the Braves raised his earned run average to a disturbing 6.20 and lowered his record to 0-4. So desperate was Berra to straighten him out that he briefly placed him in the starting rotation before returning him to the bullpen. So desperate was McGraw to straighten himself out that he elicited the help of motivational speaker Joe Badamano, who uttered the words that would become a rallying cry for his pupil and the entire club. "Joe kept saying, 'You've got to believe in yourself,'" McGraw recalled. "If I didn't *believe*, I could never do it. I had to stop worrying, start thinking positively. You gotta believe. That's it, I guess, you gotta *believe*."[2]

The new Mets mantra took hold at what became a rather divisive team meeting called by Grant on July 9. He rambled on in what amounted to a pep talk, assuring that management still believed in the players and Berra, whose job had been rumored to be in jeopardy. He spoke about the impact of injuries. McGraw grew bored, so he interrupted Grant and began bouncing from one locker to the next. He grabbed his fellow Mets and started yelling, "Do you believe? Ya gotta believe!" Some of his teammates laughed, but Grant considered the outburst disrespectful. He marched away, prompting McGraw to approach Grant and unruffle his feathers. The minority owner threatened to trade the veteran reliever if he did not begin saving games and a season quickly circling the drain.[3]

McGraw and the Mets continued to flounder. They could have packed it in, with injuries as an ideal excuse. They had lost Mays, Staub, Jones, young outfielder John Milner, and catcher John Grote at various points. But when they regained their health and McGraw found his groove in late August, they embarked on a tear worthy of the 1969 Mets. McGraw saved 12 games while allowing only four earned runs in his last 41 innings that season.

The Mets methodically cut into their deficit. They won 13 of 18 to shrink it to 2½ games heading into a do-or-die 10-game stretch against East rivals Chicago, Pittsburgh, and St. Louis in mid-September with Seaver, Stone, and Matlack clicking on all cylinders. Two straight defeats of the Pirates shrunk it to 1½ games. They waged an epic battle against Pittsburgh on September 20 with first place in their sights. The game was tied at 3-3 in the thirteenth inning when Pirates pinch-hitter Dave Augustine blasted a Ray Sadecki pitch off the top of the wall. Jones, who had smashed two home runs to lead the Mets to a victory the day before, sprinted after it. He played the carom perfectly and fired the ball to Wayne Garrett, who nailed Richie Zisk at the plate to maintain the tie. Catcher Ron Hodges, who had applied the tag, soon singled in the game-winner. Seaver shackled Pittsburgh the next night to not only place the Mets at .500 for the first time since late May but vault them to the top of the East.

There they stayed the rest of the year. Their spot on the lofty perch remained precarious—one scenario could have played out in which five teams finished the year tied for first—but the Mets won when needed. They clinched the division crown with a 6-4 victory over the Cubs at Wrigley Field on the last day of the regular season. The hero was McGraw, who rescued a shaky Seaver with three one-hit shutout innings. Wrote beat writer Jack Lang after witnessing the post-game celebration, "McGraw kept yelling, 'You gotta believe!' and even Grant, who was also in the clubhouse, did not mind it now."[4]

It would take more than believing for the Mets to win the pennant. Most considered them shark bait against powerful Cincinnati in the National League Championship Series. The Reds had won eight of 12 head-to-head matchups against New York and featured at least four position players superior to anyone wearing a Mets uniform, including future Hall of Famers Johnny Bench, Joe Morgan, and Tony Pérez, as well as Pete Rose, a first-ballot certainty had he not gambled away the opportunity. And though Seaver ranked atop all pitchers in the series, the Reds boasted plenty of depth on the mound with four starters who had compiled earned run averages of 3.51 or lower.

Two bromides about playoff baseball indicated a different outcome. One is that the team that gets hot at the right time often wins the series. The Reds had ripped off a 53-20 run to put away the rest of the West but had all but clinched by mid-September and played .500 to close out the year. The Mets remained hot and razor-sharp until wrapping up the division crown on the last day of the season. The second is that great pitching most often conquers all in the playoffs, and the Mets starting trio of Seaver, Koosman, and Matlack trumped the Cincinnati threesome of Jack Billingham, Don Gullet, and Ross Grimsley. Indeed, Berra could start Seaver twice if the series extended past three games. Nary a Reds starter could compare with the right-hander about to win his second Cy Young Award.

Indeed, the Mets ground the Big Red Machine to a halt. They limited Cincinnati to an average of 1.6 runs and six hits in five games, never scoring more than two in any of them. The difference in starting pitching talent became most evident when the Mets pounded Billingham for five runs over four innings in Game 5 to sew up the pennant. A four-run fourth in which even the 42-year-old Mays contributed an RBI single—his first hit since August 29—doomed the Reds. Soon thousands of fans among the sellout crowd at Shea Stadium stormed the field to celebrate with their baseball heroes and take pieces of sod and the fence with them. "I'm so stunned I could scream," exclaimed Mets owner Joan Payson.[5]

She would certainly have screamed had her Mets beaten the defending world champion Oakland Athletics in the World Series. But the A's were not the Reds. They could match the Mets starter for starter and closer for closer with 20-game winners Catfish Hunter, Ken Holtzman, and Vida Blue in the rotation and Rollie Fingers in the bullpen. And they too boasted far superior hitting, having led the American League in runs scored, powered by World Series MVP and could-have-been-Met Reggie Jackson, who had already begun to earn his reputation as Mr. October.

Not that the Mets went down meekly. Koosman placed them on the verge of Miracle II when he blanked Oakland in Game 5 to give his team a 3-2 series lead. But Jackson single-handedly upended Seaver two days later, then the A's delivered a third-inning knockout of an exhausted Matlack in Game 7 to win their second of three consecutive World Series championships.

Seaver spoke wistfully about what his team had achieved. He believed even in defeat that there was victory. "If you told me two months ago that we'd even be in the World Series, I'd have told you that you were crazy," he said.[6]

Indeed, many reflect historically on the 1973 Mets and claim them to be the worst Series representative ever. But their defeat of the powerful Reds and a near-upset of the Athletics paints a different picture. It shows a club that simply took a while to find itself. Once they gained their health and confidence, they were transformed into a worthy World Series participant. The "Ya Gotta Believe" mantra had rocketed them to heights once unimagined.

CHAPTER SEVEN

From Contention to Collapse

METS MANAGEMENT WAS NOT ONE TO REACT TO SUCCESS WITH CHANGE. It left what it perceived well enough alone after two World Series appearances in five years. One could certainly understand the logic had a lack of hitting not remained a problem throughout that period and ever since the team expanded into existence.

The Mets ranked eleventh among 12 teams in runs scored despite the late burst in 1973. The offensive formula was not working. The club opened the following season with much of the same core as the Miracle Mets. Starters still wearing the uniform included catcher Jerry Grote, shortstop Bud Harrelson, third baseman Wayne Garrett, and left fielder Cleon Jones, as well as utility players Ken Boswell and Ed Kranepool. Critics of the Met management mindset suggested that stud hurlers Tom Seaver, Jerry Koosman, or Jon Matlack would prove to be eye candy for trade partners that could ship back hitters to bolster the lineup. But the other side argued that a team could never have enough pitching.

The Mets proved it in 1974. They certainly needed their Big Three when George Stone fell like a stone after a 12-3 campaign to win just two of nine decisions, post a 5.07 ERA, and fall victim to a shoulder injury in July. But general manager Bob Scheffing was his own worst enemy. The big bounce-back of Stone the previous year was reportedly followed by offers for the pitcher in exchange for such notable hitting standouts as Joe Torre, Jimmy "The Toy Cannon" Wynn, and centerfielder extraordinaire Paul Blair. But the stubborn Scheffing simply stated, "We won with pitching. I'm not going to break up this pitching staff."[1]

That pitching staff struggled to overcome the meager offensive output in 1974. Only a front-office shakeup after the club posted its worst record in six years at 71-91 brought a change in philosophy. Scheffing retired after the season, and the Mets promoted farm director Joe McDonald, who had begun his career as a ticket-taker at Ebbets Field. He promptly declared there to be no untouchables. McDonald got busy beefing up the lineup—and achieved his goal without unloading Seaver, Koosman, or Matlack. He landed the hard-hitting 34-year-old third baseman Torre from St. Louis for reliever Ray Sadecki, purchased the contract of all-or-nothing slugger Dave Kingman, and received catcher John Stearns and veteran outfielder Del Unser in exchange for the inconsistent McGraw.

Little did anyone imagine that McGraw would remain a viable closer for eight more years and hang around the majors until the age of 40. But Stearns provided stability equal to that of Grote and a more productive bat. The newcomer earned four all-star berths over a six-year period with the Mets.

Where there was little stability in the mid-to-late seventies was at the helm. The club had employed just four managers from its inception through 1974, then six more handled the job over the next 10 years. Berra lost his in early August 1975 despite a decent 56-53 record. And though Grant claimed the firing was unrelated to a feud between Berra and Cleon Jones, that deteriorating relationship certainly did not help.

The beginning of the end occurred when Jones remained in Florida after 1975 spring training to rehab his knee following surgery. On May 4, he was charged with indecent exposure when found by police in a van with a woman. The Mets ordered him back to New York to apologize publicly to the media, with his wife in the room. The humiliation was deemed necessary to save the image of the franchise.

Jones returned to the lineup in late May and was platooned against left-handers by Berra. What Jones considered a second humiliation—he had even played full-time in the Hodges platoon system and had remained productive through 1974—caused him to rebel. He refused to take the field in a July 18 game after being called upon to pinch-hit. The *Sporting News* explained what happened next: "There was a shouting match between [Jones and Berra] on the bench and ended with Jones flinging his glove down, pulling towels off the rack and storming up the runway to the clubhouse."[2]

Berra claimed the incident to be the most embarrassing he'd ever experienced as a manager. He suspended Jones and told management there was no room for both of them on the team. Jones nixed two potential trades as a 10/5 player and was soon released. But Berra was not spared. He was fired on August 6 following a five-game losing streak and replaced by coach Roy McMillan. "It's a decision that has been going through our heads for some time," Grant said. "It had nothing to do with failing attendance, dissension on the team, the recent . . . turbulent problem we had over Cleon Jones."[3]

Deals to bolster the offense provided only mild and temporary improvement. Torre served as a part-time player with the Mets after 12 seasons as a full-time starter and even winning NL MVP honors in 1974. He could still hit for average—he batted .307 in 1976—but the power numbers that began dissipating with St. Louis continued to dive. Such was not the case with Kingman, who bashed 73 home runs in 1975 and 1976 combined. But he provided nothing else. He struck out at a prodigious rate, posted on-base percentages well under .300 both seasons, and proved subpar on defense at first base or in the outfield. Unser compiled a .294 average in 1975, a career-best as a full-time player. But his contributions were limited. He brought neither speed nor power to the lineup and was traded to Montreal in July 1976 for Jim Dwyer, who managed to play 18 seasons in the big leagues without ever earning more than 241 at-bats.

The Mets were spinning their wheels. Exacerbating their problems in the seventies was an unproductive farm system. Only rarely did hitting or pitching prospects earn starting spots. Potential standouts performed well briefly before fading. Among them was outfielder Lee Mazzilli, a native New Yorker who arrived in 1976 and improved annually to the point where he landed on the NL All-Star team in 1979. He appeared on the verge of national stardom in 1980. Mazzilli played with abandon, and his rugged attractiveness during the disco era prompted comparisons to John Travolta. He was even offered a role on the hugely popular sitcom *Laverne & Shirley*. Only a weak arm that motivated a move to first base seemed to prevent him from gaining the status of a five-tool player.

The Mets got the best of Lee Mazzilli's career before he faded into mediocrity.

But Mazzilli hit the wall in 1981. Elbow and back problems contributed to a collapse at the plate just two years after he had signed a five-year, $2.1 million contract that was the richest in Mets history at the time. The reacquiring of Kingman and acquisition of superstar slugger George Foster before the 1982 season seemed destined to limit Mazzilli, which at the still-tender age of 27 he refused to accept. He was soon dealt to Texas in a fruitful deal that landed right-hander Ron Darling, who thrived for the rest of the decade as a steady starter and even finished fifth in the National League Cy Young balloting to play a key role in the 1986 World Series championship season.

Such glory felt eons away for the Mets in the late seventies. Their future seemed a bit brighter after manager Joe Frazier, who had won *Sporting News* Minor League Manager of the Year in 1975, guided the club to an 86-76 record in 1976 despite glaring inconsistencies. But even then, cracks were showing. Matlack complained to Frazier about King-

Ron Darling became a mainstay in the rotation and in the run to the 1986 World Series championship.
© JERRY COLI/DREAMSTIME

man's seeming lack of interest in improving his fielding. The manager replied that he preferred not to confront the slugger "because he pouts."[4]

The situation worsened early in 1977. The team lost 21 of 27 games to fall to 15-30. Frazer was fired in May and replaced by Torre, who suffered the most among all Mets managers of the era from a lack of talent. The team had fallen apart, physically and emotionally. Seaver, Kingman, and Matlack wanted out. And they all got their wishes. Only Matlack, whose ERA soared and whose record fell to 7-15, lasted the entire season. He, too, was dealt as part of a blockbuster four-team deal that also sent the disappointing John Milner packing and netted aging slugger Willie Montañez, who led the Mets with 96 RBI in 1978 before he also faded and was shipped away.

The instability and decimation of the rotation that left the 35-year-old Koosman as its ace gave Torre, who had zero experience as a coach or manager, no chance to succeed. A lack of run support by the lowest-scoring offense in the National League caused the left-hander to lose 20 games in 1977. He followed with a 3-15 record in 1978 before he was mercifully dealt to Minnesota. Koosman rebounded to win 20 for the Twins and remain viable into his forties. But Met fans weren't complaining. The trade netted southpaw reliever Jesse Orosco, an eventual bullpen mainstay and premier closer who helped the club blossom into a champion.

In the meantime, fans abandoned a team they once supported amid their woes. These were not the lovable losers of the sixties. There was no Marv Throneberry or Choo-Choo Coleman to adore sentimentally. The Mets of this era were simply rotten. They finished last in the NL East every season from 1977 to 1983. And fans stayed away in droves. The Mets ranked among the top half of National League clubs in attendance every year from 1963 to 1976 and even paced them all each season from 1969 to 1972. But they placed in the bottom third every year but one during their slide in the late seventies and early eighties, finishing last twice.

The attraction was gone. The Mets no longer boasted talent with whom fans could identify. They came and went quickly. Their premier players year-to-year proved to be mere flashes. Mazzilli was not alone

All-or-nothing slugger Dave Kingman bashed 73 home runs for the Mets in 1975 and 1976 combined but racked up 288 strikeouts.

among them. Pitcher Craig Swan led the league with a 2.43 ERA in 1978 and followed with a strong 1979, and then he faded badly. Outfielder Steve Henderson proved to be the crown jewel in the Seaver trade, but that wasn't saying much. He hit for average but little power before the Mets used him to lure back the blast-or-bust Kingman, who proceeded to twice lead the league in strikeouts.

The Mets were acting out their own version of the movie *Groundhog Day* in the late seventies and early eighties. They were playing out the same campaign every year. They amazingly won between 63 and 68 games in six of seven seasons. The only exception was 1981 when a labor dispute wiped out more than a third of the schedule as the team was on pace to win 65.

But within that stunning sameness came change. The most impactful shift occurred at the top in 1980 when the franchise was sold to publishing giant Doubleday & Company and minority partner Fred Wilpon, who had played high school baseball with pitching legend Sandy Koufax. Wilpon and Nelson Doubleday Jr., who negotiated the deal, embraced a hands-off philosophy, allowing those they hired to do their jobs unfettered. But they toiled successfully to find the right combination in front-office personnel. Their most immediate and astute move was hiring Frank Cashen as general manager. Cashen had gained success as head of baseball operations for the dominant Baltimore clubs of the sixties and early seventies.

Cashen went to work. He grew impatient with the constant losing and fired Torre before the 1982 season in favor of George Bamberger, who had coached the Orioles and gained a reputation for teaching and maximizing the potential of young players before managing the once-woeful Brewers to a late-seventies turnaround. Cashen yearned to bolster what had been a Sahara-dry farm system.

He had already begun to make progress well before canning Torre. The Mets were destined for more misery that Bamberger would not survive before enjoying a renaissance. But those lean years would also bring hope. A youth movement was about to begin.

CHAPTER EIGHT

The Kiddie Corps

PERHAPS THE UNVEILING OF ANY PROMISING METS PROSPECT IN THE late seventies should have prompted a parade down Fifth Avenue. It was that rare. And nary a one that arrived in a big-league uniform evolved into a consistent all-star. The result was a Mets franchise spinning its wheels and a half-decade of misery for its fans.

Then it happened. It was more of a flood than a trickle. The farm system came alive soon after Frank Cashen grabbed the reins as general manager in February 1980. The payoff began on September 2. That is when 24-year-old Mookie Wilson made his debut for the Mets. Little could anyone but Cashen have imagined that the first appearance of the speedy, base-stealing centerfielder would signal the start of a new era. Talented third baseman Hubie Brooks, who had rocketed through the system after starting at Double-A, debuted two days later, and the Mets were finally flashing some potential.

That pair, along with reliever Neil Allen, who arrived in 1979, proved catalysts in the push toward contention either as active participants or trade bait. Allen spent three seasons as a viable closer before Cashen swapped him in 1983 for first baseman Keith Hernandez, whom the Cardinals mistakenly assumed, based on one year of sliding numbers, was reaching the downside of a career that once highlighted Most Valuable Player honors. Hernandez rebounded to become one of the steadiest, most productive, and finest all-around players in Mets history. Brooks left two years later in a steal of a deal that netted perennial all-star catcher Gary Carter, who gave his new team three tremendous seasons

Keith Hernandez proved himself as one of the steadiest and most productive Mets hitters of all-time.

before fading. Wilson stuck around for 10 years to become one of the most beloved players to ever wear a Mets uniform and their all-time stolen-base leader until José Reyes shattered his mark.

Cashen did not bat 1.000. His most damaging faux pas involved 1976 second-round pick Mike Scott, who showed limited strikeout potential in the minors. He bounced from Triple-A Tidewater to the Mets and regressed in 1982 after a decent 1981 season. Cashen complained that Scott was "just trying to be mediocre."[1] Scott years later offered that he "didn't really have any mentors with the Mets" and that he likely required a change of scenery.[2] The charge seemed unusual given that manager George Bamberger and coach Bill Monbouquette had earned reputations for developing pitchers.

Scott got his wish in December 1982 when he was sent to Houston for mediocre hitter Danny Heep in a deal Cashen and the Mets would certainly regret. Scott became an early disciple of pitching coach Roger Craig, learned the split-finger fastball, and skyrocketed to greatness after two mediocre seasons with the Astros. He compiled an 86-49 record from 1985 to 1989, blossomed into a prolific strikeout pitcher, and won the National League Cy Young Award in 1986.

The occasional dud by Cashen could not outrank the shrewd deals. He twice included average starter Walt Terrell to land upgrades. He traded for Terrell in a 1982 swap of Mazzilli that also brought Darling to New York. Then he shipped Terrell to Detroit after the 1984 season for unproven third baseman Howard Johnson, who eventually emerged as one of the greatest power hitters in franchise history.

Meanwhile, the standouts that would eventually lead the Mets to a World Series championship continued to arrive. It took shortstop Wally Backman more time to blossom—he made his major-league debut at age 20—but in 1984, he had proven himself a high-average hitter with stolen-base prowess and a steady glove.

By that time, two others who made immediate and powerful impacts had been promoted from the minor leagues. The first was power-hitting outfielder Darryl Strawberry, the product of Cashen's first right decision as the Mets' general manager. Cashen had to choose between Strawberry and fellow high school outfielder Billy Beane as the first overall pick in

Darryl Strawberry about to uncoil the classic swing that resulted in 335 career home runs.

the 1979 draft. Beane seemed more focused and driven; Strawberry had twice quit his team after being disciplined for lack of hustle. But Strawberry's physical tools were off the chart. Phillies scout Hugh Alexander called him "the best prospect I've seen in the last [30] years" while Mets counterpart Roger Jongewaard begged Cashen to nab him, stating that Strawberry had "greatness written all over him."[3]

Cashen indeed selected Strawberry over Beane, who lasted long enough for the Mets to snag him later in the first round and gained greater fame as the innovative, analytics-driven general manager of the Oakland Athletics who inspired the book and movie *Moneyball*. The 21-year-old Strawberry brought his sweet swing to the still-woeful Mets in May 1983 after a sizzling start in Triple-A that prompted cries from fans and the media for his promotion. Cashen preferred not to rush him but realized he needed to attract crowds to Shea. Strawberry did not disappoint, slamming 26 home runs to win NL Rookie of the Year honors.

A year later, 19-year-old right-hander Dwight Gooden took baseball by storm, compiling a 17-9 record and 2.64 ERA, placing second in the Cy Young Award balloting and giving the Mets their second consecutive Rookie of the Year. It remains one of the finest rookie seasons in baseball history.

Though the individual contributions from the farm system seemed to come methodically one year at a time, the blossoming of the Mets happened in one stunning season. And it was no coincidence that it occurred in 1984, the year Davey Johnson was hired as manager. Cashen had been Baltimore general manager when Johnson starred as an all-star second baseman for the Orioles. Johnson won three league championships as a minor-league skipper and was guiding Triple-A Tidewater when he got the call.

The GM would not regret it. He marveled at Johnson's tactical skills. "Davey makes moves in a game that are so good they are absolutely eerie," Cashen said in 1986. "Other managers are thinking of the moves they'll make this inning. Davey is thinking of the moves he'll make three innings from now. He's like [legendary Orioles manager] Earl Weaver: He's a manager for all seasons and situations. If he's eight games in front,

Dwight Gooden rocketed to stardom in the mid-1980s before his demons derailed a potentially Hall of Fame career.

Davey Johnson guided the Mets to the crown in 1986.
© JERRY COLI/DREAMSTIME

he plays it one way. If he's eight games back, he plays it another way. He adjusts. He has a sense of the moment."[4]

The improvement was indeed immediate and dramatic. The 1983 Mets finished 68-94 while ranking last in the National League in runs scored and a lowly eighth in team ERA despite a cameo from Tom Seaver, who returned to serve as ace of a lousy rotation at the age of 38. The 1984 club performed little better statistically. They ranked eighth in both categories and were actually outscored by their opponents on the season yet won 90 games. The difference was Johnson, whose in-game strategies Cashen came to appreciate. The Plus-12 difference between actual victories and Pythagorean expectation based on run differential ranks among the best ever in Major League Baseball.

Had the Mets been able to beat the eventual Eastern Division champion Cubs, they might have stunned the sports world by landing in the playoffs. They won 36 of 50 games during a midseason stretch that ended with a 2-1 defeat of the Cubs behind Gooden at Shea Stadium before a throng of 51,102 on July 27 to increase their hold on first place to 4½ games. But they lost the last three of that series and were swept four straight at Wrigley Field soon thereafter. The Mets hung around the periphery of the race until a September collapse, but the experience of a pennant race and confidence gained proved valuable. And the fans certainly responded. Home attendance in 1984 soared to over 1.8 million, the largest total since the pennant-winning year of 1973 and an increase of more than 700,000 from the previous year.

Optimism heading into 1985 appeared justified. The emergence of hard-throwing Hawaiian southpaw Sid Fernandez, whom Cashen had stolen from the Dodgers in an off-season deal in 1983 and made an impressive run in the second half of the season, added to the hope that the Mets would remain a contender. So had the trade that landed Carter and the promotion of right-hander Roger McDowell to pair with the already established Orosco in the bullpen. Waiting in the wings was starting pitcher Rick Aguilera, who had zoomed through the minor-league system and seemed ready to make an impact. "I'm comfortable with the talent here now," Johnson said two weeks before the regular season. "I didn't know what to expect from a lot of these players when I came here. Now I do."[5]

What he expected and he got was a lineup that, for the first time in franchise history, truly struck fear in the hearts of opposing pitchers. Powered by a quartet of Carter, Hernandez, Strawberry, and still-productive George Foster, the 1985 Mets ranked third in runs scored and home runs. Meanwhile, both their rotation and bullpen boasted talent and depth equal to the more celebrated 1969 staff as Gooden embarked on one of the greatest seasons ever fashioned by a major-league pitcher. Darling compiled a 16-6 record, and Fernandez rebounded from a poor spring that landed him in the minors to earn a promotion, post a fine 2.80 ERA, and strike out more than a batter per inning. It was no wonder with Gooden and Fernandez in the starting five that the Mets led the NL in strikeouts.

Lefty Sid Fernandez displays the form that made him a consistent contributor for ten seasons with the Mets.
©JERRY COLI/ DREAMSTIME

Brilliance both behind and at the plate made Gary Carter one of the premier players in Mets history.

There was just one problem. The National League East was no longer a division of pushovers. Particularly problematic was St. Louis, which provided stiff competition from beginning to end. A mediocre first half of the season punctuated by a three-game sweep at home against the Cardinals in which the Mets scored a mere three runs forced them to play catch-up. They played it well, winning 15 of 17 with an offensive explosion rarely achieved by previous Mets teams. They averaged seven runs per game during that stretch, which they completed by scoring a combined 31 in two victories over Atlanta. They remained scorching hot. Another 15-2 stretch into mid-August vaulted them ahead of the Cardinals, and the teams remained nip-and-tuck into the final week.

The Mets had a chance to complete a sweep in St. Louis and deadlock the race at the top on October 3. They banged out 13 hits—including five from Hernandez amid boos from Cardinals fans who once cheered him—but left 10 runners on base in a 4-3 defeat that all but doomed them to second place despite a 98-64 record. "It's no longer in our hands," lamented Johnson. "Now, we need help. This is our toughest loss of the season. Our destiny is out of our hands."[6]

The Cardinals clinched the East two days later. But the Mets had emerged as a power. So had Gooden, but storm clouds had already been gathering on what could have been a Hall of Fame career.

Chapter Nine

Fighting Greatness

Sprinkled in among thousands of seasons compiled by pitchers in baseball history are those so rare and dominant that they are spoken about with reverence. Walter Johnson in 1913. Lefty Grove in 1931. Bob Gibson in 1968. Greg Maddux in 1995. Pedro Martínez in 1999.

Between Gibson and Maddux, there was Dwight Gooden in 1985. The difference was age and experience. Gooden was just 20 years old when he fashioned one of the greatest years of all time. He won the triple crown of pitching, leading the National League in wins with 24, earned run average at 1.53, and strikeouts with 268. He also topped the circuit with 16 complete games.

Major-league pitchers find it nearly impossible to remain locked in from Opening Day to October. The mechanical and mental requirements necessary to achieve such a feat are overwhelming. One unintentional alteration in a delivery can result in a slump that can kill confidence. It happens to almost every pitcher every year. But it did not happen to Gooden in 1985. He allowed more than three runs in just one of 35 starts and hurled eight shutouts. He won 14 consecutive decisions from late April to late August. He surrendered no earned runs over 42 innings to start September.

So devastating was the break on his curve that it was referred to royally as "Lord Charles" rather than the colloquial "Uncle Charlie." And hitters certainly could not focus on waiting back on the curve lest Gooden fire his 98-mile-an-hour fastball by them. To put it simply, he was locked in.

"It was almost surreal, like an out-of-body experience," Gooden recalled in a 2015 article in *Sports Illustrated*. "Every game I felt totally in control. I could put the ball where I wanted it. I could throw my curveball in any count. I knew how to set up hitters. I knew I had a plan and how I wanted to attack.

"Knowing I could throw it anywhere I wanted any time, before the hitter even gets in the box I've got him defeated. That was a great feeling. About 10 starts into that season, I knew the year was going to be something special. Each time I went to the mound I wanted to pitch a complete game and I wanted 10 strikeouts. I'm not disrespecting other players, but I knew there were extra fans in attendance and they wanted to see a show. The best way to explain it is it was like a concert. And I was the main attraction."[1]

Indeed, the Mets drew an average of 6,000 more fans in the 18 games Gooden started in 1985, making his $450,000 salary quite a bargain. But Gooden had been the main attraction on the diamond since the age of nine, two years after learning the overhand curveball that would frustrate so many major-league hitters. His father, Dan, who toiled operating a conveyor belt in a phosphate factory near their Tampa home, pushed and prodded his son into working toward a baseball career. Dad cleared out a lot near their house so Dwight could practice his pitching, though the youngster preferred playing in the field and performed as a third baseman and outfielder (his hero was Tigers legend Al Kaline) in his early little-league days. Dan worked with him on various aspects of the game. So advanced did Dwight become that he played a significant role in his age 10-14 team qualifying for a Little League World Series in which he could not compete because he was too young.

The elder Gooden lived vicariously through the achievements after his own baseball dreams had been dashed. And wife Ella did not appreciate the pressure placed on Dwight, whose future outside the sport she believed was being threatened. She worried that her socially awkward son needed to be playing with his peers and making friends rather than spending hours a day mastering a breaking pitch. She felt furthermore that Dwight needed to nurture other talents on which to build a career in case baseball did not pan out. Dan even refused to allow Dwight to take a menial job like the other neighborhood boys because it took time away from his pitching. "Why are you pushing him like that?" Ella asked her husband. "It ain't his fault you didn't make it in baseball." Dan replied with an insistence that their son would indeed thrive as a ballplayer.[2]

One might assume that the ballfield became a sanctuary for the child, given a turbulent upbringing. His parents planned on divorcing after his mother, whose nurturing ways of parenting Dwight almost bordered on smothering, nearly murdered Dan after discovering an adulterous relationship. She followed her husband to a rendezvous with his girlfriend with a gun and began firing. A bullet nicked Dan's arm, but he simply drove home rather than tend to his wound at a hospital, and the couple amazingly remained together. Dan continued to play a positive role in Dwight's baseball career. Criticism of the unrelenting push of his son toward that goal can be considered justified. But it can also be rightfully claimed that Gooden would never have reached it without the urging from dad.

So advanced was the curve that complimented his blurry-fast heater at baseball factory Hillsborough High School—he struck out 130 in 74 innings as a senior—that major-league scouts took notice, and college offers began flooding in. He had begun to follow the exploits of Dodgers wunderkind Fernando Valenzuela, a left-hander who, at age 20, had taken baseball by storm. Gooden yearned to do the same. The Mets snagged him fifth overall in the 1982 draft and signed him to an $85,000 bonus. The 17-year-old initially received the typical amount given to a prep prospect with an assignment to Rookie League Kingsport, where he allowed just one home run and fanned 66 in 65⅔ innings to earn a promotion.

He was merely warming up. Gooden landed at Class A Lynchburg in 1983 and produced one of the most dominant seasons in minor-league history. Gooden proved willing to accept and apply coaching advice. He had been simply blowing away hitters with his fastball, but Lynchburg pitching coach John Cumberland understood the need to use it to set up his entire repertoire by buzzing them inside. Gooden took the guidance and ran with it. He compiled a 19-4 record with a 2.50 ERA and an outrageous 300 strikeouts in 191 innings. Though the embracing of Cumberland's pitching philosophy caused his walk ratio to rise, Gooden proved virtually unhittable. He had punched his ticket to the big leagues, incredibly bypassing Double-A and Triple-A in the process (though he did pitch at the latter level in playoff competition). "He's a baby," Cumberland said. "But he also isn't a baby. At 18, he's got the poise (Nolan) Ryan had at that age. And 10 times the control."[3]

Gooden showed a desire to stay grounded by calling his parents and sisters after every outing at Lynchburg. It became apparent he would soon be making calls from the Big Apple. He was impressing the right people, including soon-to-be Mets manager Davey Johnson, who had been serving as manager at Triple-A Tidewater after a stint as roving minor-league instructor.

"I saw Gooden pitch for two or three weeks, and said, 'This is the best pitching prospect I ever saw,'" recalled Johnson in 1984. "And I saw [Hall of Famer] Jimmy Palmer when he came up with the Baltimore Orioles."[4]

Johnson wanted Gooden promoted to Tidewater before Lynchburg had concluded its 1983 season. That did not happen until Gooden pitched a shutout to clinch the Class A pennant and the Tides began their playoffs. He proved himself ready to thrive one level below the big leagues. He struggled in his first start with Tidewater but impressed Johnson with his desire to learn. "I told him not to worry about it," Johnson remembered. "He said, 'I got behind in the count, and then gave them pitches that were too good.' I thought, 'He not only has good stuff, he knows what he's talking about. He's always learning. He reads the hitters exceptionally well for any age. He pays attention.' He pitched again, went nine, beat Richmond. He pitched again, went nine, beat Denver. He was 18 years old. . . . I said, wherever I'm managing in 1984, that kid will be my opening day pitcher."[5]

Little did Johnson know that he would be managing the Mets in 1984. Johnson was philosophically opposed to rushing pitchers to the big leagues, but he suggested that general manager Frank Cashen be open-minded about Gooden joining the club to start that season. The Mets were not only desperate for pitching but also to lure fans after ranking dead last in National League attendance in 1983. Gooden did not fulfill Johnson's promise of starting Opening Day, but he earned a spot in the rotation and debuted by defeating Houston. He lacked consistency in his rookie year, following a few strong starts with a dud. But he allowed just two runs in his last 34 innings in 1984 and placed first in all but one Rookie of the Year ballot. Only a 16-1 season by Cubs right-hander Rick Sutcliffe prevented Gooden from winning the Cy Young Award as well.

Gooden and the rejuvenated Mets had brought a ray of sunshine to a city of darkness. New York remained a crime-ridden metropolis with a murder rate that had started skyrocketing a decade earlier and would continue to rise a decade later. Gang wars over crack cocaine had infiltrated Queens street corners near Shea Stadium and furthered an epidemic that had gripped the nation. Gooden indeed helped provide a welcome diversion and sense of optimism. But grim reality resulted in the opposite. New York City in the eighties was not the ideal place and time for a Dwight Gooden who had yet to celebrate his twentieth birthday.

Temptation and negative influences certainly did not affect Gooden in 1985. He toyed with the greatest hitters in the world. When his father asked him to strike out 16 Giants in an upcoming start, he struck out 16 Giants and shut them out to boot. He belied the notion that nobody that young could be that dominant. He contradicted what seemed to be proven that hitters eventually catch up to pitchers the more they face them. Perhaps both remain facts—but his stuff was simply too good. Yankees scout Stan Williams offered that Gooden could break Cy Young's record of 511 career victories. And the great Sandy Koufax, who compiled arguably the greatest five-season run of any pitcher in baseball history? "I'd rather have his future than my past," he stated in all seriousness.[6]

One would have assumed such unprecedented success was bringing joy to Gooden. But one would have assumed wrong. He spoke decades later about feeling the pressure after every brilliant outing to follow it up with another.

"Looking back, I don't think I enjoyed it as much as I should have," he said. "It was a game, but it's a job. I was so locked in from start to start that I wasn't truly aware of what was going on even after games that I won. Now I have a 10-year-old son, and sometimes we'll be watching one of those games from '85, and it's almost like watching somebody else. He'll say to me, 'Wow. You were 20 years old. You must have been happy.' And I would tell him, 'Where's the joy on my face?'"[7]

The emotional burden and fear of failure played a role in Gooden increasing his alcohol intake in 1985. Soon, he found a pressure valve in a more sinister form. Three months after a season in which he nearly carried the Mets to the pennant, he was hanging out with his cousin, who left the house in Tampa to score some marijuana. Gooden poured some vodka while waiting for his cousin to return, then opened the bedroom door to find two half-naked women making out. They invited him in to watch and try some cocaine. He first declined—he was a drinker, but the white powder represented a boundary he preferred not to cross. Then he crossed it while downing the vodka.

"At first, I thought it was the finest feeling I ever had, though it was a false feeling," Gooden recalled. "The first time I tried cocaine . . . the best way to say it is this: It was the worst mistake of my life, at [21] years old."[8]

Gooden rejected the notion that the comparative unavailability of cocaine in smaller major-league cities such as Kansas City would have altered what became a dangerous path. He offered instead years later that the lure of women and sex triggered a desire for cocaine and that combination can certainly be addictive. Federal drug trials in 1985 revealed the extent of cocaine use among ballplayers. Included was Mets teammate Keith Hernandez, who compared cocaine to the devil, and claimed to have quit.

Gooden was never the same. Though no pitcher could have maintained the same level of dominance as he did in 1985 throughout a career, the negative trappings of an eighties lifestyle for the rich and famous doomed a pitcher with Hall of Fame talent to a slowly disintegrating career. The Mets rewarded Gooden in the off-season by signing him to a one-year, $1.32 million contract, making him the youngest millionaire in major-league history. Supposed friends came out of the woodwork in Tampa to take advantage. The result was that he surrounded himself with those who did not have his best interest at heart.

Trouble started immediately. He hurt his ankle shagging fly balls with friends and kept the injury a secret from Mets brass as spring training was about to begin. An anonymous caller informed Cashen of the injury, which Gooden then claimed was the result of a jog on a high school field. He told Cashen he would return to New York immediately to have it examined, then instead engaged in a lithograph signing in Manhattan and flew back to Tampa. Later that spring, he claimed falsely to have been in a minor accident and too emotionally distraught to pitch to get out of an exhibition start. The warning signs were ignored by the Mets brass. So was his poor spring in which his ERA soared to over 4.00.

Pitching coach and former Yankees standout Mel Stottlemyre added fuel to the fire. He tinkered with the reigning Cy Young Award winner. Stottlemyre, who had earned a fine reputation with the Mets, decided Gooden needed to add a change-up and two-seam fastball to a simple variety that included just a fastball and curve. When Stottlemyre talked, pitchers listened. And Gooden was not one to rebel, so he dutifully worked on doubling his repertoire. Catcher Ed Hearn could barely believe his eyes when he caught Gooden in the bullpen and saw him toying with the two-seamer. "I'm thinking, *What the hell is this?*" Hearn remembered. "He was a power pitcher with tons of movement, and they're trying to teach him *movement*? What the hell for?"[9]

The result was a flawed delivery that negatively affected Gooden's performance. His release point changed from one pitch to the next. Pitching had come naturally to Gooden. The alterations forced him to think too much about his motion on four different pitches. Catcher Gary Carter even offered that Stottlemyre's insistence that Gooden expand his number of offerings played a role in shoulder problems he later developed.

In 1986, more among the Mets' hierarchy chimed in. Cashen admonished him to lower his leg kick to prevent base stealers from getting a good jump. Assistant general manager Joe McIlvaine suggested that he not try for strikeouts but rather pitch to contact so he could save his arm. Gooden had been a strikeout pitcher since joining the professional ranks, but he listened to Stottlemyre. He listened to Cashen. He listened to McIlvaine. He yearned to please one and all.

The result in 1986 was far from catastrophic. Gooden still went 17-6 and fanned 200 in his role as ace of a World Series champion. But his ERA nearly doubled, and he followed a strong playoff effort with two early-knockout defeats in the World Series. And, like many of his Mets teammates, his debauchery that included heavy cocaine use increased. Gooden celebrated the ultimate triumph by embarking on a party-till-dawn cocaine binge. He even missed the team victory parade, watching it instead at his drug dealer's apartment in the projects of Long Island.

The downward spiral continued. He was arrested in December for fighting with police and failed a drug test early in spring training in 1987, forcing him, at the team's urging, to enter the Smithers Alcoholism and Rehabilitation Center in New York City, a stint that cost him two months of the regular season and failed to cure him of his cocaine addiction. He also remained a heavy drinker. Only his incredible talent allowed him to overcome his problems to stay effective on the mound.

Gooden was good enough for the rest of his Mets career, but the kid who seemed destined for the Hall of Fame fell victim to a shoulder injury in 1989 that eventually required surgery, needed tremendous run support to compile a 19-7 in 1990, and deteriorated into a .500 pitcher thereafter. The Mets understood by 1993, after allegations surfaced that he and two teammates had raped a woman in Florida, that he would never return to the form that made him a sensation. But they supported him anyway. "There is an almost universal affection for him," said general manager Al Harazin. "For us, he represents the best of the '80s, a symbol of that success."[10]

The end of his days in a Mets uniform was near. He gave flash-in-the-pan outfielder Tuffy Rhodes his 15 minutes of fame by surrendering three home runs to him on Opening Day 1994. The failure to start the season so angered Gooden that he kicked a bat rack and broke his toe. The injury required a rehab assignment, during which time he fell back into a cocaine habit. He was suspended for 60 days by Major League Baseball, then suspended again for the entire 1995 season after another positive test. He never again wore a Mets uniform.

Gooden hung on thereafter like so many journeymen as team after team—including the Yankees in 1996 and 1997 and again in 2000— hoped against hope that he would rediscover the magic on the mound. That never happened (though he did hurl his only career no-hitter in May 1996).

Far more important was his battle for sobriety. It didn't happen, at least up to July 2019, when he was twice arrested, once for cocaine possession and six weeks later for driving under the influence.

His downfall ranks among the greatest tragedies in baseball history. There would be no more Cy Young Awards. There would be no Hall of Fame enshrinement. The career of Dwight Gooden would forever be marred by substance abuse and scandal. But memories of his brilliance before they were diminished by the scourges of cocaine and alcohol can never be erased.

Chapter Ten

1986

Mets general manager Frank Cashen treaded lightly before the 1986 season. Why tinker with greatness? The club boasted an elite offense for the first time in its history. Its production meant a deep rotation spearheaded by standouts Dwight Gooden, Ron Darling, and an emerging Sid Fernandez needn't be broken up by trade. And the 1-2 bullpen punch of blossoming right-hander Roger McDowell and co-closer Jesse Orosco consistently finished what the starters started.

Cashen did make one splash—though it barely caused a ripple when consummated. He acquired heretofore mediocre lefty Bob Ojeda, a players-rights firebrand who angered veteran teammates and Red Sox management, in a deal that sent promising reliever Calvin Schiraldi to Boston. Soft-tossing southpaws most often do not thrive in Fenway Park. But one could not have imagined the positive impact Ojeda would make on the Mets, particularly in the special season to come.

The 1986 Mets took a no-holds-barred approach to hedonism. But they felt they had every reason to be loose and cocky. They were loaded—on and off the field in different definitions—and they knew it. They stormed out of the gate, battering all in their path, and ran away with the National League East despite a bit of a comedown season from Gooden. They won 11 straight to end April and seven more in a row early in May. They took 10 of 11 in early June to extend their division lead to 11½, and it was game, set, and match. The Mets were relentless even after their clinching what became as inevitable as the sun rising in the east. They finished on a 15-4 run to conclude the regular season with a franchise-best 108-54 record.

Every cog in the offensive wheel ran to maximum efficiency. Veteran catcher Gary Carter exceeded 100 RBI for the third consecutive year. Young slugger Darryl Strawberry took another step forward and slammed 27 home runs. Hitting machine Keith Hernandez batted .310 and drew a career-high 94 walks. Third baseman Ray Knight enjoyed his finest season since 1979. Second baseman Wally Backman hit a shocking .320. And sparkplug center fielder Lenny Dykstra compiled an on-base percentage of .377 to garner some MVP attention in his first full season. Outfielder Mookie Wilson maximized more sporadic playing time.

The rotation proved rock-solid and downright brilliant from beginning to end. The quintet of Gooden, Darling, Ojeda, Fernandez, and Rick Aguilera started all but 14 games and combined for a ridiculous 76-30 record. Orosco and McDowell saved 43 between them as the Mets posted the lowest team ERA in the sport.

Who was the second lowest? It belonged to none other than the Astros, a surprise team that entered the playoffs against the Mets a heavy underdog. Most clubs offer at least faint praise to opponents heading into a postseason showdown. Not the 1986 Mets. They showed utter disdain for a Houston club with a starless lineup that finished in the bottom half of the league in runs scored. Never mind that first baseman Glenn Davis was a prolific slugger and his teammates pecked opponents to death with singles, stolen bases, and clutch hitting. And even the NL champs could not scoff at a deep Astros rotation that featured still-dominant Nolan Ryan and a fine relief corps.

That rotation was anchored by none other than Mike Scott, who was sent away three seasons earlier in a rare Cashen mistake and emerged as an ace. But the Mets questioned how Scott dominated. Even manager Hal Lanier failed to strongly reject the validity of protests that his ace scuffed the ball to add late movement. After all, he offered, Scott had never been caught cheating. Carter held a far different opinion, one gained through experience. He recalled a Scott pitch during the All-Star Game that fell off the table. "I checked the ball, and it was scratched," Carter declared. "I mean, scratched big time."[1]

Intriguing side stories abounded as the Mets and Astros prepared to battle for the pennant. One that involved Scott—sort of—resulted

Lenny Dykstra faded in the late 1980s for the Mets before gaining stardom in Phila-delphia.

from a July 19 incident outside what has been described as a "kind of cooler disco type" of Houston bar called Cooter's, which allowed celebrities to booze it up for free. Scott had shut down the Mets that night in an Astros victory, and an unruly, drunken quartet of Aguilera, Darling, Ojeda, and typically well-behaved second baseman Tim Teufel got into a scuffle around closing time with off-duty police. The Mets later claimed that Teufel was jumped by a cop and that his teammates merely sprang to his defense. Darling was pushed into a glass door and shattered it as all four were arrested and spent the night in a holding cell. They were also fined by the team for breaking curfew, not that such debauchery was foreign to this club. But the event did heighten hatred among Astros fans for their team's soon-to-be playoff opponent. Cooter's took advantage of the well-publicized confrontation by selling T-shirts that read, "Houston Police 4, Mets 0."[2]

No matter. The Mets made no pretense of respect for their upcoming foe. Asked in what areas his team boasted an edge, Strawberry answered, "The team."[3]

The Astros played more like a bunch that was angered by the dismissive mindset of their opponent than one intimidated by its talent. And it was Scott who set the tone for a highly competitive series by reminding Cashen with his right arm that he had erred by trading him. He required only a Davis solo home run to outduel Gooden in Game 1 at the Astrodome with a five-hit shutout that included 14 strikeouts. The Astros had made it apparent to the Mets that they were in for a fight. Ojeda worked out of jam after jam in Game 2 for a 5-1 victory that sent the clubs back to Shea Stadium deadlocked.

The rest of the series was a donnybrook. Each game was a taut test of wills and abilities to rise to the occasion with a World Series berth on the line. Dykstra played the hero in Game 3 with a pinch-hit, two-run homer in the ninth inning off super-closer Dave Smith to wrest victory from the jaws of defeat. Davey Johnson had rolled the dice and won despite his hitter taking an approach at the plate he despised. "Dykstra does like to swing for the fences. I tell him all the time: 'If you hit line drives, you'd hit .330 every year. But I forgive him today," said Johnson. He had won that round of the individual battle against Houston counterpart Hal Lanier, who edged him out for National League Manager of the Year honors.[4]

There was just one problem—and that was Scott awaiting his Game 4 start. He stymied New York in a complete-game, 3-1 victory that tied the series at 2-2 and had the Mets once again charging their former team-mate with scuffing baseballs. The Mets needed a triumph the next night. A defeat that would require successive victories in Houston threatened doom. The Astros were downright deadly in the Dome with a 52-29 regular-season mark. An epic pitching duel ensued between a new stud and an aging one. Gooden and Ryan, who fanned 12, each allowed one run over 19 combined innings. Carter grounded a game-winning single up the middle in the twelfth to send his team to Texas on the verge of a pennant.

Among the Mets who understood the importance of winning Game 6 was Knight. He gave his team no chance to beat Scott in Game 7 at the Astrodome. The Mets tried to convince National League president Chub Feeney that Scott had been scuffing baseballs for effect by holding on to one and presenting him with Exhibit A but to no avail. Feeney declared Scott innocent until proven guilty and stated such a conclusion had yet to be drawn. Now the Mets dreaded the prospect of facing Scott for all the marbles. "If we face Scott in Game 7, we lose," Knight stated plainly. "I hate to say that, but it's true. We don't go to the World Series."[5]

Neither the fans at the packed Astrodome nor the millions watching at home could have anticipated that two teams that had engaged in such a stressful series were about to take the tension up a notch. One of the greatest games in major-league history ensued. Not that such drama appeared likely throughout. Houston standout southpaw Bob Knepper protected an early 3-0 lead like a father protecting his baby. He mowed the Mets down inning after inning. A Game 7 showdown with Scott, who was in their heads and waiting in the wings, appeared inevitable when the Astros took that same advantage into the ninth inning. Knepper's pitch count was under 100, and he was rolling merrily along.

Then it happened—though Knepper didn't know why. He offered that maybe he ran out of gas. Or maybe he lost his focus. Or maybe it was a combination of both. But the Mets started belting him all around the lot. Dykstra tripled. Wilson singled him in. Hernandez doubled in

Wilson to knock out Knepper and summon closer Dave Smith. Carter and Strawberry walked. And Knight tied it with a sacrifice fly.

What followed was a titanic struggle as the Mets fought for the NL crown and the Astros fought for their lives. McDowell mowed down batter after batter for five scoreless innings, prompting a Stottlemyre concerned about his pitcher's availability for a possible Game 7 to ask Johnson, "How long are you gonna go with Roger?"[6] His teammates couldn't score for him until the fourteenth, when hits by Carter and Backman plated the go-ahead run. The Mets were on the precipice of the pennant as Johnson replaced McDowell with Orosco, but the lefty faltered, allowing a home run to Billy Hatcher in the bottom of the inning.

The teams played on. And that gave Knight a chance to play hero again in the sixteenth. He followed a Strawberry double with a run-scoring single to knock out aging right-hander Aurelio López, not the same reliever who had dominated American League hitters for years in Detroit. A walk, two wild pitches, and a Dykstra single stretched the lead to 7-4 and seemed to put the pennant away.

But Orosco was running on fumes. Johnson was taking no chances with lesser relievers. He told his lefty that he was going to win it or lose it with him on the mound. Orosco allowed four of five batters to reach base as the score tightened to 7-6. Up to the plate stepped Kevin Bass, who had hit .311 that year and had remained one of the hottest hitters in the series. Hernandez recalled that Orosco had thrown a fastball to Hatcher that had tied the game, so he paid his teammate a visit. "Jess, I don't give a fuck what Gary calls," he said. "If you throw this guy one fuckin' fastball, I will kill you."[7]

Bass saw five sliders, the last of which he swung through. Game over. Pennant won. The Mets were emotionally exhausted. "I have never played with such intensity," declared Hernandez. Added Knight: "I've never been involved in anything so emotional or been under such mental strain."[8]

Nobody could have believed such a physically, mentally, and emotionally draining event would be followed by another. The 1986 World Series has not been deemed by many the greatest of all time because it lacked drama.

Red Sox–Mets. The anticipation of this World Series would be rich with storylines. Any battle between Boston and New York—never mind that the Yankees were uninvolved—was destined to draw tremendous attention. And it did. More than 1,100 media types around the world received credentials to cover the event.

Subplots abounded. There was a spotlight on the Ojeda-Schiraldi trade. The former had performed far above expectations in 1986 while the latter emerged as a bullpen stud after a long stretch at Triple-A Pawtucket and a conversion from starter. Then there was the Sox' 68-year championship drought since the infamous selling of Babe Ruth to the Yankees, otherwise known as the "Curse of the Bambino." Last but not least, was the showdown between Dwight Gooden and Red Sox ace Roger Clemens, who most outside New York believed had passed his rival as the greatest young pitcher in baseball. While Gooden regressed that season, Clemens burst onto the scene by compiling a ridiculous 24-4 record, recording the first 20-strikeout game in major-league history, and winning the Cy Young Award at age 22.

Even the respective city mayors got involved. New York mayor Ed Koch, who didn't know the strike zone from the *Twilight Zone*, bet Boston counterpart Ray Flynn that the Mets would win the series. Koch would receive baked beans and New England clam chowder for a New York victory and would send apples and corned beef sandwiches in the event of a Mets defeat.

The Sox had emerged from a championship series even more dramatic than the one that had vaulted the Mets into the ultimate title round. They had trailed the Angels 3-1 and were down 5-2 in the ninth inning of Game 5 before rebounding remarkably to win, then clobbering their foe twice at Fenway.

Both World Series combatants arrived at Shea Stadium with momentum and confidence. But a rare backfired decision by Johnson played a role in getting his team off on the wrong foot. He decided to start Teufel over Backman at second base against Boston left-hander Bruce Hurst, who embarked on a shutout while Darling did the same into the seventh. With one on and one out in the top of that inning, Boston catcher Rich Gedman stepped to the plate. The old high school nemesis of Darling hit an easy grounder to second. "As soon as he hit it, I thought, 'Wheeew, I'm out of this mess,'"[9] recalled Darling. But he wasn't. Teufel raised his glove anticipating a bigger bounce, and the ball scooted underneath it. Red Sox 1, Mets 0. And that was the final score.

Teufel spent the next 24 hours in emotional torment. He called committing such a faux pas to lose his first World Series game a "nightmare."[10] He was attacked by the media and excoriated by fans on sports talk shows. And even team chaplain Dan Murphy threw a nasty backdoor curve at a sermon attended by Teufel before Game 2. "None of us will be here next week because we'll all be celebrating," Murphy said. "But in life you win and you lose. Some days you're Bruce Hurst and some days you're Tim Teufel."[11]

And some days, you're Roger Clemens or Dwight Gooden. The two studs were duds that night in what proved to be among the biggest pitching-matchup letdowns in World Series history. A national television audience of 65 million watched what had been billed as an epic duel quickly dissolve. Clemens and Gooden combined to allow eight earned runs on 13 hits and six free passes in 9 ⅓ innings. Johnson allowed Gooden to hit with two on and two out in the fourth despite his team trailing, 4-2, drawing boos from the Shea faithful. But it likely didn't matter. The Red Sox pounded Aguilera as well while their bullpen mowed down the Mets in a 9-3 victory that sent the series back to Fenway and had baseball fans pondering a sweep.

It also had Mets fans pondering what could have been. Their team had selected Clemens in the twelfth round of the 1981 amateur draft out of San Jacinto Junior College, but a workout for then-manager Joe Torre and pitching coach Bob Gibson prompted the latter to urge the Mets not to overspend. They offered Clemens a signing bonus of just $25,000, which he rejected in favor of a scholarship from the University of Texas. Cashen had since lamented the mistake in judgment in the knowledge that his team could have boasted both Gooden and Clemens in its rotation.

Two home defeats plummeted the Mets to rock bottom in their quest for a crown. But the friendly confines of Fenway heated up their bats. Their offense transformed from ice cold to scalding hot. They averaged

5.8 runs and 10.6 hits per game the rest of the way. Nearly every hitter contributed, and several took turns playing hero. Ojeda and Darling shut down the Sox on three runs in Games 3 and 4 combined while Dykstra and Carter racked up 10 hits, four home runs, and nine RBI between them to tie the series at 2-2. Neither team had won a home game.

That soon changed. What did not change was the struggles of Gooden, whom Johnson decided to pitch on three days' rest while Boston manager John McNamara held back Clemens for Game 6 with a rested Hurst ready to roll. Hurst again performed brilliantly, blanking the Mets over the first seven innings while placing himself on the precipice of a series MVP award and his team on the brink of its first title since 1918 while Gooden was sent to the showers after allowing three straight hits to start the fifth. His team battled back late, but Hurst fanned Dykstra, who represented the tying run, to end it.

The Mets were on the doorstep of doom with Clemens itching to pull the trigger at Shea. A parachutist named Michael Sergio lightened the mood when he descended upon the field early in the first inning of Game 6 to the amusement of both teams and the delight of the sellout crowd. But that served only as a temporary break to the tension. The prospect of the wunderkind suffering from successive poor performances seemed dim. They dimmed to darkness when Ojeda allowed two runs on five hits in the first two innings, and Clemens began mowing down the Mets. He faced just 13 batters and fanned six of them to take a 2-0 lead into the fifth.

It seemed only intervention from Lady Luck could save the Series. And she was clearly wearing a Mets uniform on this night. She had already signaled her arrival when Jim Rice failed to score from first on a two-out double in the first inning. She further came to the rescue when Clemens popped a blister on his pitching hand to help the Mets score two in the fifth to tie the game. The injury that caused blood to flow from his right index finger eliminated the slider from his repertoire and limited him to fastballs and forkballs. Clemens wasn't long for the outing. A torn nail sustained in the seventh resulted in bleeding from two fingers. He remained effective enough, however, which explains the controversy over his removal for a pinch-hitter in the eighth after he had retired the Mets in order with a 3-2 lead.

McNamara insisted for years thereafter that Clemens had asked to be removed. The fiery superstar claimed the opposite. The consensus was that McNamara was lying. Hurst offered that Clemens was far too fierce a competitor to ask out of a World Series game, particularly one in which the Red Sox could clinch their first crown in 68 years. *Sports Illustrated* reported that Clemens was furious at being taken out of the game. Either way, it could be perceived as another example that Lady Luck had bets riding on the Mets.

Soon, another mini-drama in the midst of a major drama arose. It came in the form of Schiraldi, who had performed brilliantly down the stretch in the regular season and the American League Championship Series before saving Game 1 of the World Series. His performance had softened the sting for Red Sox fans from the off-season trade of Ojeda, who had pitched far better in a Mets uniform. Schiraldi had emerged as a bit of a cult hero, but one wondered if at age 24 with little major-league experience he could rise to the most pressure-packed occasion a pitcher could face.

He didn't. Perhaps the heat of the moment overwhelmed Schiraldi or McNamara had failed him by keeping him sidelined for a week. But he was simply not the same pitcher who had struck out nine Angels in 6⅔ innings in the ALCS or fanned Danny Heep to end the opener. He faced 11 batters in the seventh and eighth combined, allowing a run that tied the game at 3-3. It appeared, however, that he would go down as the winning pitcher when the Red Sox battered Aguilera in the tenth for two runs to place themselves on the verge of a historic World Series triumph.

Then Schiraldi arrived on the mound with a gas can. That did not surprise the Mets who knew him. Most had played alongside Schiraldi. They did not perceive him as a pitcher who could withstand pressure once it reared its ugly head. "I love Cal, but I told the guys the truth," said Mets backup catcher Ed Hearn. "If we're able to get to Schiraldi, he does not have the makeup to be a stopper. He's not psycho enough to come in late, and he gets on himself too much. We can beat him up-and-down."[12]

Now the Mets needed to beat Schiraldi up-and-down to avoid a Series defeat. The tension had become unbearable. Not only were they battling the Red Sox for their very lives, but they were also battling themselves. Strawberry became so angry when he was removed by Johnson for defensive purposes after the ninth inning in favor of Mazzilli that, in a stunning show of selfishness and injured ego, Strawberry stormed out of the dugout and into the clubhouse to pout. The move even made sense beyond defense—Strawberry had made the last out in the eighth anyway.

Hollywood scriptwriters would have tossed what happened next in the garbage can as implausible. As celebration champagne was rushed to the Boston clubhouse, Schiraldi appeared to have righted himself. He retired Backman and Hernandez to start the eleventh. The Diamond Vision scoreboard operator mistakenly flashed "Congratulations Red Sox!" on the screen. The faux pas proved, to say the least, premature. Boston pitcher Dennis "Oil Can" Boyd didn't think so. He mocked the Mets by waving goodbye to them from the dugout.

The Mets did not wave back—they fought back. Carter singled to left. Kevin Mitchell singled to center. Carter thought Schiraldi looked scared, an emotion the younger pitcher denied. What he could not deny was that he was tired as he was about to face his sixteenth batter in less than three innings. McNamara could have replaced him with veteran Bob Stanley, who had hurled 6⅓ shutout innings in the series. But he stuck with Schiraldi. And he was about to pay the price. Up to the plate stepped Knight, seeking not only to keep his team alive but also to atone for a critical error in the seventh that allowed the Red Sox to forge ahead. And he did by blooping a single to center that cut the deficit to 5-4.

McNamara could wait no longer to summon Stanley, who, like Knight, was seeking redemption. He had, after all, lost his closer role to Schiraldi in a brutal August. To save the series would prove the ultimate personal restitution. He assumed all that stood in his way was Mookie Wilson. Little did he know catcher Rich Gedman proved a more fatal, though unintentional, adversary. With the Red Sox one strike from a crown, Gedman failed to move his body to flag down an inside palmball. It hit off the outside of his glove and rolled to the backstop as Mitchell sprinted in for the tying run. The die was cast. One could sense the life being sucked out of the Red Sox. The Curse of the Bambino felt all too real.

The moment Mets fans, Red Sox fans, *baseball* fans would never forget was at hand. It would be replayed as often as any play in the history of the sport. The joy of victory and agony of defeat for all to see. Wilson sent a simple bounder to first baseman Bill Buckner, who had been hobbled by leg injuries throughout the playoffs. Hindsight is 20/20, and McNamara certainly regretted not removing him in favor of younger and steadier Dave Stapleton. Buckner raised his glove a few inches to where he assumed it would bounce next. But it flattened out and scooted underneath. Knight scored. Bedlam ensued on the field and in the stands. The Mets had saved the Series.

Lady Luck had once again intervened. Now it was the turn of Mother Nature. Rain forced the postponement of Game 7. The delay seemed to favor the Red Sox. They could now start Hurst for all the marbles rather than the eminently beatable Oil Can Boyd, who was furious at the snub and charged the organization with racism. McNamara later claimed that Boyd got himself so drunk he could not pitch in relief in Game 7.

The bit of good fortune from a pitching standpoint appeared to have paid off for the Red Sox as Hurst cruised into the sixth inning with a 3-0 lead, courtesy of a three-run third off Darling, who was removed an inning later for lights-out Sid Fernandez.

The Mets never lost their confidence. Three singles, including a two-run hit by Hernandez, and a groundout in the sixth tied the game at 3-3. "Even when they led, 3-0, we felt we could get to [Hurst]," said Hernandez. "And once we got to their bullpen, we felt we had it."[13]

The Mets certainly had Schiraldi's number. If McNamara believed a day's rest was all he needed to return to form, he had another think coming. Knight provided the rude awakening with a leadoff home run. Two singles later, he was gone, but that did not stop the Mets from scoring three runs and taking a 6-3 lead. The Sox battered McDowell for three straight hits to close the gap to 6-5 in the eighth, but Orosco shut them down. Then Strawberry put the cherry on top with a massive blast to right off Al Nipper, the fourth pitcher McNamara had used in one full inning as he futilely searched for an effective alternative.

Strawberry lollygagged around the bases, savoring his moment of perceived vindication for the perceived slight when Johnson removed him from Game 6. When he finally reached home plate, he was stopped by the veteran Knight, who gave him some fatherly advice. "Ray has a lot more experience than I do," Strawberry recalled. "He said to me, 'OK, you've just shown what you can do again, now be a man and don't rub it in, don't say anything more. Go shake hands with Davey. Put it behind you.'" Strawberry did just that, exchanging high-fives with his manager as he reached the dugout.[14]

Soon, they would all be exchanging high-fives and hugs and bubbly. Orosco had polished off the Red Sox in the ninth, and the Mets had won their second championship. And Wilson, who had lived through the bad old days that really weren't old at all, expressed his feelings. "I know what it's like to be in the cellar, to be home during this time of year watching the World Series with a pizza and beer. I really don't know what I'm thinking right now."[15]

New Yorkers did. An estimated 2.2 million attended the Parade of Champions in Lower Manhattan the following day. Several players, including Hernandez and Ojeda, barely made it after nights of heavy drinking. Gooden was in such a stupor he failed to show up at all. It was

The Mets celebrate their 1986 World Series championship.
© JERRY COLI/DREAMSTIME

typical Mets. Even Johnson, when asked if the baseball fans of America would fully appreciate what his team had accomplished, was forced to admit they would not because "the bad guys won."[16]

Indeed, they had. But when it was time to play baseball, no team was better in 1986.

CHAPTER ELEVEN

When Great Was Not Good Enough

EXPANDED DIVISIONS AND WILD CARDS WERE MERE TWINKLES IN BASE-ball's eye in the late eighties. The powers-that-be remained steadfast in their belief that regular-season crowns should remain a holy grail in battling for playoff positions. Only four of 24 teams reached the postseason.

The lure of big bucks from television revenue and late-season gate receipts had yet to grow strong enough for Major League Baseball to embrace a watered-down playoff system that allowed .500 teams to stay alive well into September and beyond. Granted, the 1973 Mets won the pennant with an 82-79 mark, but that was an anomaly. From 1974 to 1995, when division playoffs were launched, only the 1987 Twins reached the World Series with fewer than 90 wins. Seven clubs with fewer than 90 victories played in the Fall Classic from 1996 to 2019.

The Mets certainly would have preferred the modern setup in the seasons following their 1986 championship. Their hitters continued to rake. Their pitchers continued to rank among the best in the National League. Manager Davey Johnson and general manager Frank Cashen continued to push mostly the right buttons. But the team would not make a return visit to the World Series until the iconic showdown against the crosstown Yankees in 2000.

Unlike the GMs of a bygone era in Mets history, Cashen did not stand still after his team claimed the crown. He allowed Ray Knight to leave via free agency in the knowledge that promising slugger Howard Johnson could take over at third base. And he dealt Kevin Mitchell to San Diego in a seven-player swap that landed outfielder Kevin McReynolds.

Johnson blossomed in 1987, even garnering some MVP votes after steal-ing 32 bases and finishing second on the team behind Strawberry in home runs (36) and RBI (99), while Knight managed one decent season in Bal-timore and faded away. Mitchell left San Diego for San Francisco, where he earned National League Most Valuable Player honors in 1989 and remained a feared, but erratic, power hitter for several years. McReynolds proved far more consistent. He averaged 24 home runs, 87 RBI, and 13 stolen bases over five seasons in New York. But teammates saw a player who lacked passion for the game and pride in wearing a Mets uniform.

Indeed, both moves worked statistically but not emotionally. Mitch-ell and Knight were among those considered the heart and soul of the 1986 team. Knight was a team leader whose departure had a negative effect on morale. And not only did Davey Johnson foresee Mitchell as a pure hitter destined for a full-time starting role but also the deal for McReynolds even had racial undertones. It has been suggested that the front office perceived Mitchell as a negative influence on Strawberry and Gooden, whose careers had begun to be plagued by substance abuse. But Mitchell was beloved by all teammates, and it seemed the only reason for such suspicion was that he bore the same skin color. "I can't make a man go in there and suck on some white powder," Mitchell said. "How can I? I ain't never used any drugs in my life. . . . I rarely even dealt with Gooden and Strawberry off the field."[1]

Attendance at Shea cracked three million for the first time in 1987 and increased the following year. The Mets remained one of the premier teams in baseball through 1990. Though his players complained about some of his personnel decisions, Cashen remained a highly effective general manager. He must have been wearing a mask when he robbed right-hander David Cone from Kansas City before the 1987 season. Cone dominated in the lower minors after the Royals snagged him in the third round of the 1981 draft. Cashen recognized his potential and somehow convinced Kansas City general manager John Schuerholz to unload him for catcher Ed Hearn and second-rate hurlers Mauro Gozzo and Rick Anderson. Cone had struggled in 1984 and 1985 after reaching Double-A, and then again as he tasted a cup of coffee in the big leagues a year later.

Howard Johnson averaged nearly 100 runs scored and RBI from 1987 to 1991.

David Cone locks in, perhaps as he prepares to fire one of his blistering fastballs.

The initial impact for Cone did not motivate him to turn cartwheels. Born and raised in Kansas City, he was looking forward to becoming a hometown hero after landing a spot in the rotation during spring training. Going to the pitching-rich Mets threatened Cone with another year in the minors. But his sidearm slider and split-finger fastball proved so impressive to pitching coach Mel Stottlemyre heading into the regular season that Cone earned his place on the roster. And fitting in with the wild bunch was no problem—he quickly realized his new teammates were an ideal fit for his friendly and rather silly personality. Hernandez, in particular, "made me feel more welcome in one day than the Royals had in six years."[2]

An injury to Bob Ojeda and Dwight Gooden checking into a substance abuse rehab center forced Cone into a starting role in late April. But he too was not long for the rotation. He performed inconsistently, then fractured his pinky finger squaring for a bunt in late May and missed nearly three months. He found his groove upon his return to help the Mets make a belated run at St. Louis for the division crown. A four-game winning streak in mid-September vaulted them to within 1 ½ games of first place after falling 10 games back in July. But the Mets faltered down the stretch with an 8-9 record to finish out of the playoffs despite posting the second-best record in the league at 90-72.

Cone and his club were ready to reestablish themselves as the Beast of the East in 1988. He headed a quintet that also included Gooden, Ojeda, Sid Fernandez, and Darling that proved the deepest and best in the sport. Cone embarked on one of the finest seasons in baseball history. Motivated greatly by his growing legion of fans, some of whom began wearing pointy head coverings and calling themselves "Coneheads" after the *Saturday Night Live* family, he compiled a 20-3 record and 2.22 earned run average. Gooden would never regain the dominance he displayed in 1985, but he pitched a full season and posted an 18-9 mark and 3.19 ERA. Meanwhile, all but Ojeda received plenty of support—the Mets paced the senior circuit in runs scored despite down years from Carter and Johnson. And an off-season trade of Orosco to the Dodgers proved to be no issue. He was replaced as co-closer (along with Roger McDowell) by emerging southpaw Randy Myers, who launched a fine career in that role by saving 26 games and posting a 1.72 ERA. It was no wonder they led the National League in attendance for the first time in franchise history as more than three million fans again streamed through the turnstiles.

A Cone shutout of Atlanta on May 3 catapulted the Mets into first place, where they remained the rest of the year. And they arrived at an NLCS showdown against the equally dominant Dodgers with momentum after concluding the regular season on a 19-4 roll.

The headline battle pitted Cone against Los Angeles ace Orel Hershiser, who had just broken the all-time record set by fellow Dodger Don Drysdale by pitching 59 consecutive scoreless innings. No pitcher has ever entered the postseason hotter. But the Mets seemed to own a psychological advantage heading into the series, having beaten them in 10 of 11 meetings. "We owned them," Darling recalled 25 years later.[3]

They didn't own Hershiser—nobody did. The sizzling ace extended his scoreless streak eight innings in Game 1 to outduel Gooden, who performed brilliantly as well despite falling behind 2-0. But the Mets kicked up their heels in the ninth on a Gregg Jefferies single and a Strawberry run-scoring double. Dodgers manager Tommy Lasorda arrived on the mound to remove Hershiser—he should have brought a cattle prod with him. Hershiser insisted he was fine and stated emphatically his desire to stay in the game. Lasorda was equally insistent on summoning closer Jay Howell, who struck out Johnson to bring his team to within one out of a victory to the delight of a roaring sellout crowd at Dodger Stadium. But Carter sent a looping liner to center on which John Shelby attempted a diving catch rather than playing it on a bounce to limit the damage. The ball scooted away as two runs scored to give the Mets a 3-2 lead. Myers blanked LA in the bottom of the ninth to secure the victory.

Soon a side story reared its ugly head. Cone had agreed to have an article about his Game 1 experiences and feelings ghostwritten for the *New York Daily News*. Among his thoughts splashed in the newspaper for all to read was that Hershiser was "lucky to go eight [shutout] innings" and that Howell "reminded me of a high school pitcher." As one could imagine, the insults did not sit well with the guys wearing those iconic blue-and-white uniforms. They placed a copy of the piece in every locker and on the clubhouse wall. The timing for Cone could not have been worse—he was set to start Game 2 in Los Angeles.[4]

He was mashed. So unnerved by the commotion created by the article was Cone that he balked a runner into scoring position in the first and paid for it by allowing a run. That was a wonderful inning compared to the second when he allowed five consecutive batters to reach to fall behind 5-0. He might not have survived the frame had he not been scheduled to lead off the third, which allowed Johnson to pinch-hit for him and avoid using a third pitcher. The Mets closed the gap to 6-3 and even brought the tying run to the plate in the ninth before succumbing to defeat.

The good news was that Cone, who admitted he'd been overcome by nervousness, learned his lesson and apologized for his lack of judgment. And his old journalism career was put on hold. The Mets knew he had placed another hurdle to overcome. "David was pretty stupid to do it; I'm sure he'll admit that," Hernandez said. "And he was a wreck. Their bench was riding him hard. Lasorda and the bench. I just had a bad feeling about that game. I wish I'd gone in and talked to him, but I don't think I could had had any effect on him. He got his butt kicked."[5]

The desired remedy was home cooking. The series moved to frigid Shea for Game 3, and the embarrassment shifted from the Mets to the Dodgers. Perhaps one could perceive that Cone gained vindication after Howell arrived to protect a 4-3 lead in the eighth. The right-hander walked McReynolds to open the inning and ran the count to 3-2 on Johnson. Davey Johnson slowly emerged from the dugout and informed home plate umpire Joe West that there was something fishy about Howell. West and crew chief Harry Wendelstedt examined his glove, detected pine tar, and the latter gave him the heave-ho. A leak eventually turned into a two-out tidal wave. Backman tied the game with a double, and then five straight Mets reached base to emerge with an 8-4 lead. Game over. Davey Johnson was taking no chances—he used Cone in the ninth to finish off the Dodgers.

The series rocked back and forth. Gooden continued to resurrect his 1985 form in Game 4 with a hitless run from the fourth to the eighth as his team built a 4-2 lead. But he allowed a two-run homer in the ninth to light-hitting catcher Mike Scioscia as the raucous Shea crowd fell dead silent. A bullpen battle broke out. The Dodgers forged ahead on a solo homer by eventual World Series hero Kirk Gibson off McDowell in the twelfth. The Mets loaded the bases with one out in the bottom of the inning. One hit would have placed them on the brink of their second championship in three years. But Orosco erased Strawberry on a popup. Then Lasorda made one of the boldest moves in World Series history. He summoned Hershiser, who had taken it upon himself to get ready, to secure the final out. Hershiser induced McReynolds to pop out as well to complete an epic 5-4 victory and knot the series.

The rest of the NLCS proved far less dramatic. Game 5 was marked by a sudden and shocking collapse of Fernandez, who mowed down the Dodgers on one hit through three innings, then surrendered run-scoring doubles to lesser-lights Rick Dempsey and Alfredo Griffin in the fourth before Gibson blasted a three-home homer in the fifth to stretch the lead to 6-0, sent Fernandez to the showers, and placed the Mets in a hole out of which they could not climb.

The result was added pressure on Cone as the series moved back to LA. Neither the Dodgers nor their fans had forgotten the article for which he was responsible after the opener. The Mets could not survive another defeat. And the game was to be played in the same ballpark in which Cone received a shellacking six days earlier. But Cone performed like the 20-game winner he had been in 1988. Backed by McReynolds, who played the role of offensive hero with four hits, including a home run, Cone hurled a complete-game five-hitter to keep his team alive. "I think the whole country saw the real David Cone tonight," McReynolds said.[6]

There was just one problem—and his name was Hershiser. He was set to start Game 7 while Johnson was forced to decide between Gooden on just two-days rest or Darling on three. He chose the latter—then wished he hadn't. Giving Hershiser a big lead was baseball suicide, and that's what Darling did. He was replaced by Gooden in a five-run second inning that was exacerbated by errors from Backman and Jefferies. The Mets barely sniffed a rally against Hershiser, who allowed just one hit in the last four innings to deny them another crown.

Cashen did not overreact to the letdown during the off-season. But he did make one unpopular move that was viewed as perpetuating the dismantling of the 1986 World Series champions. He traded Backman to Minnesota for three minor leaguers destined never to play a major-league game. The trade made sense statistically—Backman was all but done, and it allowed Jefferies to secure full-time duties at second base. But it did not ingratiate Cashen to the fans or teammates. Backman was considered a scrappier player than Jefferies, who was perceived as preferring not to get his uniform dirty.

Jefferies had been touted as one of the greatest prospects ever to wear a Mets uniform, and he certainly believed he would live up to the hype. He even bragged he would eventually become the all-time leading hitmaker in Major League Baseball, stating, "When I see Pete Rose on TV and he gets a hit, the announcers always say how many hits he has now for his career. I hope he keeps building on it because I'm going to beat that record."[7]

The Mets gave Jefferies the cold-shoulder treatment. The problem became so acute in 1991 that he sent a message through sports talk radio that he would like to be given the same level of support from teammates that he provided them. The plea was received like a spikes-high slide into second. Jefferies was further alienated, leading to a trade to Kansas City along with McReynolds before the 1992 season for declining, injury-plagued right-hander Bret Saberhagen, who eventually wore out his welcome as well with a series of clubhouse pranks. Jefferies performed better after leaving, eventually garnering National League MVP votes with St. Louis and emerging as a consistent .300 hitter, albeit with less production than once predicted of him. But McDowell claimed that the Mets didn't miss him. "Gregg Jefferies killed us," he said. "He was treated as an outcast because he was an arrogant kid who thought he was better than everyone else. Other than wearing a uniform, he was not part of that club."[8]

The breakup of the 1986 Mets continued after a disappointing start to 1989 in which they had sunk to .500 in mid-June. That is when Cashen pulled off a deal that again alienated fans and teammates. He sent McDowell and centerfielder Lenny Dykstra, perhaps the most popular

Mets player, to Philadelphia for veteran second baseman-turned-outfielder Juan Samuel. Cashen had played one card too many. Samuel performed terribly and was shipped after the season to the Dodgers for fading first baseman Mike Marshall, who also struggled in the Big Apple. Meanwhile, Dykstra blossomed with the Phillies, twice leading the NL in hits and finishing second in the MVP vote in 1993 after pacing the league with 143 runs scored and helping his team win the pennant. Though Dykstra fell victim to substance abuse and other legal problems that led to multiple arrests following his playing career, he remained one of the most popular players in franchise history.

Another key contributor to the championship year departed in July. Pitcher Rick Aguilera was shipped to the Twins along with promising right-hander Kevin Tapani in July in exchange for reigning American League Cy Young Award winner Frank Viola. What Cashen and vice-president of baseball operations Joe McIlvaine likely did not imagine was that Minnesota would transform Aguilera into one of the premier closers in baseball while Tapani emerged as a standout starter who played a significant role on a club that would win the 1991 World Series. Viola, a Mets fan growing up and standout pitcher at St. John's University, won 20 games as ace of the staff in 1990, but bone spurs in his elbow contributed to a collapse the following year before he signed a free-agent contract with Boston. A deal that received much fanfare turned out to be a dud.

The 1989 Mets hung around the pennant race into September. But it had become apparent that a team that once hoped to be a dynasty was instead heading in the wrong direction. The death blow was soon to come.

Chapter Twelve

Goodbye Davey, Hello Misery

THE AX FELL ON JOHNSON IN 1990. HIS CLUB HAD FALLEN UNDER .500 at the end of May for the first time since 1983 when Cashen replaced him with third-base coach and former Mets shortstop Bud Harrelson. Johnson was deemed too lax in his discipline, though few complained about him when his players were running around at all hours of the night four years earlier. But what is fine when winning is not fine when losing, and Cashen perceived the team as an undriven underachiever. Harrelson promised to instill a sense of passion.

Among those applauding the move was veteran pitcher Ron Darling, who had bickered with Johnson in 1990 about stints in the bullpen and had been angered a few days previous when the manager refused to order retaliation after Mets batter Kevin Elster had been plunked against San Diego. Some players felt they had let Johnson down. Darling spoke about the respect he and his teammates had for Johnson. But he also hoped Harrelson would lay down the law. "The rules have been there," he said. "What Buddy is going to do is what the government would call a strict interpretation of the rules. I think he is really going to hold to curfew. There will be no more golf and no more playing cards. There will be a tightening of the reins. On the field. Off the field. Everywhere."[1]

The Mets responded—but it took some time. They lost four of five and then caught fire. Their white-hot bats fueled a 25-4 stretch in which they averaged an incredible 6.9 runs per game and vaulted from 8½ games back to a half-game out of first place. They allowed a mere 28 runs during an 11-game winning streak in which Gooden, Cone, and Viola

Seen here showing off his bunting skills, Bud Harrelson both played for and managed the Mets.
© JERRY COLI/DREAMSTIME

combined to win all seven of their decisions. Among the highlights of the tear was a comeback walk-off win over old friend Roger McDowell and the Phillies that completed a sweep in front of nearly 50,000 fans at Shea Stadium.

The good times did not last. The Mets barely played over .500 baseball the rest of the season. They flirted with a division title until they had a devastating five-game losing streak in mid-September from which they could not recover. More changes were forthcoming. Vice-president of baseball operations Joe McIlvaine, considered the heir apparent to Cashen as general manager and a major factor in personnel decisions, bolted after the 1990 season to take the GM position with San Diego, citing warmer climes and what he claimed to be a better place to raise his kids. Cashen followed McIlvaine out the door, retiring a year later as

McIlvaine replacement Al Harazin took over the front office as general manager. But he too resigned in January 1993.

By that time, the team could have been called the New York Mess. One of the most potent lineups in baseball had been downgraded significantly by 1991. The final significant piece to the 1986 machine was Darryl Strawberry, who had decided when Johnson was fired that he would leave in free agency and indeed took the big bat that was overshadowed by drug, legal, and back problems to the Dodgers and was waived himself after three miserable seasons. The Mets might have owned the weakest offense in the National League that year if not for Howard Johnson, whose 38 home runs represented one-third of the team total.

Not that the season proved disastrous from the start. They scored enough runs in its first half to allow the rotation triumvirate of Frank Viola, Dwight Gooden, and David Cone to thrive. The Mets even won 10 straight to open July and move within 2½ games of first place. But what followed was an unforeseen and epic collapse that would send the club into a tailspin that would last five years and claim the stints of five managers. An 8-27 stretch that included an 11-game losing streak during a horrific road trip all but doomed Harrelson, who was fired in what proved to be the final move by Cashen, and replaced by third base coach Mike Cubbage with a week left in the season.

The manager that promised greater discipline had not delivered it. One player stated anonymously that Harrelson "spent the whole season managing like he was everyone's pal, and that doesn't work."[2] But he certainly had not earned their respect. Viola responded to the dismissal by stating it should have happened months earlier.

What had become apparent to Harazin was that the Mets required a more commanding presence. So he hired Jeff Torborg, who had won AL Manager of the Year honors with the White Sox in 1990 and guided them to another fine season in 1991, yet suspected that new GM Ron Schueler was forcing him out. Torborg hightailed it to New York. It was a move he would come to regret.

The Mets needed someone who could manage egos and inspire, two issues typical for the most expensive club in the major leagues with a $45 million payroll. The front office had tried to buy and trade its way back into contention.

Their first foray into the era of free agency proved disastrous. They signed former St. Louis super-stealer Vince Coleman to a four-year contract for nearly $12 million before the 1991 season. But the same speedster who swiped a ridiculous average of 92 bases in six years with the Cardinals never played a full season for the Mets as injuries and punishments cost him 215 games. One problem followed another on and off the field. He ignored or misread base stealing signs. He engaged in a verbal battle with Cubbage, which factored into the dismissal of Harrelson. A physical confrontation with Torborg in September 1992 resulted in a suspension. He injured Gooden's arm the next April by recklessly swinging a golf club in the clubhouse. He annoyed teammates by laughing after losses. And, in the coup de grace that finally bought his ticket out of the Big Apple, he threw a lit firecracker into a crowd of fans waiting for autographs outside Dodger Stadium, injuring three (including a two-year-old girl) and received 200 hours of community service. He had to go despite failed attempts to trade him. Coleman was finally unloaded to Kansas City in January 1994 in a swap that returned Kevin McReynolds, who played sparingly for one final season before retiring.

The flurry of moves continued after the signing of Coleman. Steady starter Ron Darling was dealt to Montreal for nondescript reliever Tim Burke. But it was the spending spree before the 1992 season that raised many an eyebrow. The Mets signed still-slugging, future Hall of Fame first baseman Eddie Murray to a two-year, $7.5 million contract. He remained a viable threat, averaging 22 home runs and 97 RBI before leaving in free agency for Cleveland. But the biggest bombshell hit a week later when the Mets inked right fielder Bobby Bonilla to a five-year, $29 million deal to make him the richest player in team sports. The staggering sum was criticized, but Harazin claimed other clubs offered Bonilla more.

Raised in the South Bronx, Bonilla was coming home. "Right place, right time," he said after signing. "It's almost a storybook. I've got a soft spot in my heart for New York. I'm going to be myself. All I can do is bring myself and my smile and have fun."[3]

Bobby Bonilla did not perform as well as he did in Pittsburgh, yet the Mets agreed to pay him big bucks into 2035.

Mets fans were not smiling for long. The move seemed wise at the time—Bonilla had nearly won the Most Valuable Player Award in each of the previous two seasons. He was an RBI machine, averaging just over 100 since 1987. He was reaching his prime and coming off arguably his finest year with career-bests in batting average (.302), doubles (44), walks (90), and on-base percentage (.391). But Bonilla proved far less productive in a Mets uniform than he had been in Pittsburgh, though a vastly inferior supporting cast certainly contributed to his declining numbers.

Bonilla began with a bang, slamming two home runs to help beat St. Louis on Opening Day in 1992, and then he went the next 39 games without going deep and finished with just 19 for the season. Though he rebounded as a power hitter the following two years, he never justified the contract, and both the fans and media responded. So loud were the boos and catcalls at Shea that he began wearing earplugs.

His toxic relationship with reporters, with whom he later admitted he should have worked harder to get along, grew worse that year when he was caught lying about trying to convince an official scorer to change an error into a hit, then threatened a *Daily News* sportswriter for calling him out. Both the Mets and Bonilla were happy to part ways in 1995 when a youth movement motivated McIlvaine (who had been rehired as GM in 1993) to ship him to Baltimore for highly touted minor-league outfielders Alex Ochoa and Damon Buford, neither of whom lived up to the billing.

Though only Coleman among the major free-agent signees completely bombed, the big spending did not produce the desired results. On the contrary, the Mets descended below mediocrity. That was not the fault of Murray and Bonilla—if not for them, the 1992 Mets might have run out one of the worst lineups in baseball history. Illness and injury had even slowed down the bat speed of Howard Johnson as pitchers chucked fastballs by him. Meanwhile, the trio of Gooden, Cone, and Fernandez remained effective, but they received little help from the offense or bullpen, and the rotation lacked depth.

Most ironic is that the Mets added power-hitting second baseman Jeff Kent as their full-time starter in 1993 and ranked significantly lower in runs scored that season. Their offense lacked versatility. They spent much of the year smashing solo homers as they placed dead last in the National League in on-base percentage. And the trade of Cone to snag Kent further weakened the mound staff. The Mets specialized in adding past-their-prime pitchers. Included in 1993 was 39-year-old southpaw Frank Tanana. Making matters worse was a horrific bullpen that consistently blew close games. It was no wonder the team's Pythagorean won-loss record, which is based on run differential, was 14 games better than the 59-103 mark they compiled on the year, their worst since the bad old days of 1965.

To the surprise of no one, Torborg did not last that season, despite the fact that they would be forced to throw away money after signing him to a four-year contract. Owners Fred Wilpon and Nelson Doubleday were demanding change, and Harazin complied, firing Torborg in late May after a 4-18 stretch in favor of former Yankees and Phillies manager Dallas Green, who had landed with the Mets as a scout. Green arrived with a reputation for treating unproven young players and veteran stars alike. He was considered tough but fair. "Dallas Green is a unique personality," Harazin said. "He will put his stamp here. I think he thinks he can turn the team around. I'm not looking for him to win 15 or 20 straight and jump us back into contention with the [first-place] Phillies. But what I want to come from the rest of the season is the sense that the franchise is back going in the right direction."[4]

That did not happen in 1993. The Mets lost 27 of their first 35 games under Green and only once won successive games until mid-July. Green failed to hit Harazin's turnaround timeline, though he did return the club to respectability during his tenure. It would take several years and the impact of another manager to transform them into a winner.

CHAPTER THIRTEEN

The Hometown Closer

SOME PERCEIVE THE CLASSIC PERSONA OF A CLOSER AS A HULKING flamethrower blowing batters away with fastballs. But Mets managers spent the first three decades of the team's existence summoning pitchers to lock up victories who did not fit that image. And nobody in franchise history served that purpose longer than John Franco.

While the Goose Gossages and Lee Smiths of the baseball world were dominating out of the bullpen with gas or devastating hard stuff, Franco was adding to the ninth-inning drama. He was making Mets fans nervous at Shea Stadium by nibbling at the corners and allowing baserunners before sending them home happy.

Franco was far from imposing on the mound at 5-foot-10 and 170 pounds. His out pitch was a circle change that darted away from right-handed batters like a screwball. He threw off the corner to lure overeager hitters. And if they refused to swing and took a walk or slammed a hit, Franco just focused on the next guy. He compiled a mediocre career WHIP (walks and hits to innings pitched) of 1.33. Sometimes, he drove Mets fans to the exits angry—Franco blew 19 percent of his career save opportunities. But his double-figure save total for 15 consecutive seasons, including 10 with the Mets, speaks of the trust managers felt for him and his overall effectiveness. He led the National League in saves three times, remained through 2020 as the all-time saves leader among left-handers in major-league history with 424 (two ahead of eventual Mets closer Billy Wagner), and pitched effectively approaching his mid-forties. Yet

John Franco shows a slight smile of satisfaction after racking up yet another save for the Mets.

he received so few Hall of Fame votes in his first opportunity that he dropped off the ballot after one year.

Though Mets fans will likely never have a chance to travel to Cooperstown to witness a Franco induction, they will always embrace him as one of their own. Franco was born and raised the son of a city sanitation worker and a tough but loving mother in the gritty Marlboro Housing Projects near the Bensonhurst area of Brooklyn. The life he led and friendships he forged there remained to him more cherished than the left arm he used to earn millions. While other ballplayers embraced the trappings of fame for social climbing and mansions, he and wife Rose continued to live in the Bensonhurst home of his parents, both of whom died tragically less than two years apart in 1987. "I could live anywhere. I've got the money," Franco told *Sports Illustrated* in 1989 while still employed by the Cincinnati Reds. "But when I walk out the door and walk around the block, everything reminds me of the good times and the bad times."[1]

His neighborhood was rocked by racial disharmony between African Americans and Italian Americans. There were muggings and rapes and knifings. Gunfire could be heard outside the 86th Street Night Gallery disco that could have been mistaken for the club in which John Travolta danced in *Saturday Night Fever* and in which Franco met Rose. The joint was nicknamed "The Shooting Gallery." Yet even the roughest play brought mindless fun to young Johnny. When he wasn't engaging in one of many forms of ball games (stickball, Wiffle ball, paddleball, etc.) with his friends, they were blindly smacking each other on dark elevators or battering one another with wrapped magazines on their forearms as they skated as if playing roller derby.

Franco was a Mets fan growing up, as his father had been since the team expanded into existence in 1962. The young boy and his buddies often gathered 20 Borden's milk cartons, as that was the number required for a free upper-deck pass to Shea Stadium. His favorite player was Tug McGraw—little could he have imagined he would eventually wear the same uniform and assume the same role as his idol.

He seemed well on his way as a senior at Lafayette High School to launching a professional career. Franco compiled a 14-1 record and averaged an incredible 17 strikeouts per game that season yet waited in vain to be selected in the amateur draft. His 5-foot-7, 140-pound frame scared away scouts and forced him to accept a scholarship at St. John's, where he and Frank Viola formed a dynamite one-two pitching punch. Franco was small but cocky and brash. Angered by the trash-talking of a Nebraska coach before an NCAA Regional game in 1979, the freshman blanked the Cornhuskers despite a 102-degree fever. And he rubbed it in along the way. "As every inning goes by, he's got a little more swagger going," Viola recalled years later. "Finally, he . . . just turns and just looks at the Nebraska dugout. He didn't show them up, he just gave them a look to let them know what's what. That was Johnny."[2]

That success did not immediately endear Franco to college baseball. He did not own a car, and the two-hour train trip from home to St. John's grew so bothersome that he told his father he wanted to quit school. Dad did not take kindly to such talk. He understood his son's potential. He used the moment as a motivational tool. Franco stayed in school and continued his ascent as a pitcher.

Major-league scouts soon learned their lesson about Franco, who went from unpicked to being selected in the fifth round of the 1981 draft by the Dodgers. That proved to be a lucky break as it allowed him the opportunity and honor to be tutored by none other than minor-league pitching instructor Sandy Koufax, a fellow left-hander who had also starred at Lafayette and then evolved into arguably the greatest pitcher in baseball history. Koufax taught his protégé the changeup that would also make him a star before the Dodgers foolishly packaged him as a throw-in to the Reds in a deal that landed the quite-less-than-immortal Rafael Landestoy.

Despite Franco allowing 336 hits in just 262 ⅔ innings and compiling an ERA over 5.00 in 1982 and 1983 combined, the lousy, pitching-poor Reds wasted little time promoting him to the big leagues and converting him from starter to reliever. And he wasted no time establishing himself as their premier bullpen option, even before he became their full-time closer. Franco compiled an 18-5 record and 2.38 ERA in his first two seasons with Cincinnati before landing the stopper spot.

Among the memorable moments of his rookie season was his first outing at Shea Stadium. It was a dream come true for the Brooklyn boy, but the reaction of Mets fans to his arrival as he was wheeled in the oversized "apple cart" to the mound proved rather disconcerting. "Getting into that cart was the worst thing I could have done," he recalled. "All the way down the leftfield line I had beer thrown at me, I had pennies thrown at me, I got called every kind of name you could think of. I felt like saying, 'Hey, I'm from New York!' But I had that different uniform on."[3]

Those catcalls would eventually turn to cheers but not until 1990 after Franco had averaged 33 saves in a four-season span with the Reds, twice led the league in that category, earned three All-Star Game berths, and even received Most Valuable Player votes in 1988. His impending free agency and the emergence of famed "Nasty Boys" Rob Dibble and Norm Charlton motivated the Reds to trade Franco to the Mets for Randy Myers before the 1990 season. Mets manager Davey Johnson believed Franco to be the most consistent reliever in the National League. It came as little surprise in February when his team signed the New York native to a three-year, $7.6 million contract, which at that time was the richest in franchise history. Franco expressed delight that he and Rose, along with 20-month-old daughter Nicole, would be spending his seasons in his hometown. And that hometown expressed delight when Franco performed at the same level he had in Cincinnati.

Franco led the NL with 33 saves in 1990 and maintained his effectiveness as one of the premier closers in the game for one of its worst teams. Franco received fewer save opportunities as the Mets took a precipitous drop from contender to bottom-feeder. He even compiled a remarkable 30 saves to again pace the senior circuit in 1994 despite pitching for a club that won 55 in a season shortened by labor strife. He continued to put batters on base and make fans nervous. But he more frequently than most completed his work by shaking hands with teammates after victories. Among the primary reasons was that he rarely allowed big flies. Franco gave up a mere 29 home runs over 513⅓ innings in his first nine seasons with the Mets. He surrendered fewer than 0.7 homers per nine innings every year but one.

The exception was 1993—and Franco had an excuse. He had lost all of July and September in 1992 to an inflamed elbow that eventually required surgery. The surgeon even asked him in wonderment how he was able to pitch at all. The problem reared its ugly head again in April the following season, causing him to miss another month. A strained rib cage killed off nearly all of August 1993 as well. Franco was not right, and it showed. The season proved to be like a blip on his career radar— an anomaly. He lost his pinpoint control. He finished the year with a 5.20 ERA that was nearly double what had been typical for him. Franco struggled to such an extent that Mike Maddux catapulted over him into the closer role.

That campaign proved difficult for Franco emotionally. Throughout his life, he had been able to consult with his father during tough times. He honored his dad by wearing a New York City Department of Sanitation T-shirt underneath his jersey. But after blowing four saves in eight appearances and surrendering 11 runs on 16 hits over 6⅓ innings during one hideous September stretch, he expressed his frustration in a tribute to dad. "Sometimes I step off and look up, to straightaway center field, and say, 'Help me out,'" Franco said. "Or I say, 'Pops, make this one a little easier.' All the time. Especially in tough situations. Sometimes it works, sometimes not. I mean, this is the first time in 10 years I've been through a tough season like this. It's tough to accept."[4]

Such seasons have done permanent damage to careers. The personal responsibility associated with frequent beatings that lose games has destroyed the confidence of many a closer, which is one reason few last long in that role. That Franco continued for years thereafter to serve as one of the premier stoppers in the sport spoke of his grittiness and the swagger for which he was admired.

Franco indeed rebounded in style. And when the Mets were ready to contend, he was ready to rise to the occasion. He continued to walk ninth-inning tightropes and sometimes fell off—he lost all eight of his decisions in 1998. But he recorded 74 saves in 1997 and 1998 combined.

And even after a finger injury that wiped out two months in 1999 and resulted in flame-throwing trade acquisition Armando Benítez assuming the closer role, he remained a central figure in playoff races and postseason victories. He pitched a scoreless inning to earn the win that closed out the Arizona Diamondbacks in the 1999 National League Division Series after Benítez had blown the save, and snagged the only Mets win in the 2000 World Series. One of his career highlights came at

Overpowering Armando Benitez wrested the closer duties away from John Franco in 1999 and maintained them until a trade to the Yankees in 2003.

age 40 in the NLCS against San Francisco when he was called upon for the save after Benítez had again blown the lead. Franco polished off the Giants in a critical Game 2 on a changeup for called strike three after falling behind 3-1 in the count against perennial MVP candidate Barry Bonds. "I've been making a living for 17 years getting people out on my changeup," Franco said. "What better time to throw it?"[5]

Injuries limited his appearances and effectiveness thereafter, but Franco remained a viable reliever well into his forties. His emotional ties to New York were strengthened following the terrorist attacks in 2001. He lost friends who were police officers, firefighters, and investment bankers working in the Twin Towers. His emotions spilled out in tears before the Mets played their first game after the tragedy. Franco became strongly engaged in charity work and youth baseball in New York.

The man who ranks third in all-time pitching appearances in major-league history with 1,119 would not sniff Hall of Fame induction. But he will be forever remembered for his tenacity and contributions on and off the field in the city that remained so near and dear to his heart.

CHAPTER FOURTEEN

Valentine's Day

METS HISTORY HAD ALREADY MADE ONE POINT AS DALLAS GREEN PREpared for his first full season as manager (though strike-shortened 1994 proved to be no full season for any team). That is, concerted efforts to build a winner through free agency resulted in far less success than positive production from the minor-league system.

The development and promotion of such standouts as Tom Seaver, Jerry Koosman, and Cleon Jones fueled the sudden rise of the World Series championship club in 1969 and beyond. The influx of talent such as Darryl Strawberry, Dwight Gooden, Mookie Wilson, and Roger McDowell had the same effect on the title-winning team of 1986 and the contenders later that decade.

Another trend had also taken form. The Mets performed worse under tough disciplinarians than they did playing for trusting, encouraging managers such as Gil Hodges and Davey Johnson, who gave every player a feeling of worth. Though they took advantage of the latter through their unbridled hedonism, it was those very problems, not Johnson, that prevented them from maximizing their potential. And though "everybody's friend" Bud Harrelson did not last long at the helm, the 1991 Mets did turn their season around when he assumed control from Johnson. The collapse did not materialize until he left.

One could not read Green heading into his tenure. He was neither overbearing nor a pushover. But he had gained a deserved reputation for treating his talent fairly. And the underachieving Mets required a manager unlike the departed Jeff Torborg, who would consistently get along with the players on what was still a veteran-laden roster.

The new face seemed to be making a difference in 1994. Green fashioned a 55-58 record seemingly with smoke and mirrors. The Mets ranked second-to-last in the National League offensively in strikeouts and on-base percentage—a deadly combination. A veteran, talent-laden lineup again failed to produce. The only exception was slugging first baseman Rico Brogna, whom the Mets had acquired from Detroit before trading him in 1996 to Philadelphia to make room for John Olerud. Brogna emerged with the Phillies as a premier run producer, albeit only for three seasons before fading. He had taken the National League by storm before the strike in 1994, batting .351 with seven home runs in just 131 at-bats.

The club also benefitted from a renaissance season from veteran right-hander Bret Saberhagen, who had changed his ways and performed like the ace the Mets hoped he still could be despite advancing age. Saberhagen had made more of a mark as a prankster than a premier pitcher in his first two seasons in New York, though knee and elbow injuries, as well as a lack of run support, certainly contributed to his mediocre numbers. "I've tried to change my habits around the clubhouse, not screw around so much," he said. "That's tough for me to do because I've always been a practical joker. But now before I do something I think of the ramifications."[1]

Saberhagen might have won 20 games had more than a quarter of the season not been lost to the work stoppage. He finished on an incredible roll after a start in which he managed a 7-4 record and 3.58 ERA. He won his last seven decisions to compile a 14-4 mark. Saberhagen sported a 1.51 earned run average during that stretch while walking only five batters in 71⅔ innings and placed third in the NL Cy Young Award voting.

The Mets of the mid-nineties were a mishmash of talent. For every promising young player such as Brogna, third baseman Edgardo Alfonzo, and pitchers Bobby Jones and Jason Isringhausen, there were two aging free agents or veterans either proving themselves as nothing more than stopgaps or simply underperforming in New York. Joe McIlvaine, who had returned from San Diego to take over GM duties from Al Harazin,

Bret Saberhagen managed one stellar season for the Mets after winning two Cy Young Awards in Kansas City.

continued to pepper the roster with such players as Brett Butler, who could still hit singles in his sleep but brought nothing to the long-term future of the club.

Optimism about that future was not piqued when Saberhagen caught fire. He was already a 31-year-old with an injury history. It was, however, when Isringhausen proved his talent upon his promotion in July from Triple-A Norfolk, where he had been tearing up the International League with a 9-1 record and 1.76 ERA. The rookie righty continued to dominate after getting his feet wet, winning eight of his last nine decisions while surrendering just 17 earned runs in 70⅓ innings.

The brilliance of Isringhausen, who placed fourth in the Rookie of the Year balloting despite making only 14 starts, sparked the 1995 Mets. They finished strong after bottoming out at 35-57. They remained inconsistent but ran more hot than cold the rest of the year with two five-game winning streaks and two six-game tears, including one on a homestand

Edgardo Alfonzo averaged 103 runs scored for the Mets from 1997 to 2000.
© JERRY COLI/DREAMSTIME

that concluded the season. The organization hoped the influx of young talent would spur badly needed interest in a club that was in the process of finishing in the bottom half of National League attendance for seven straight seasons while reducing payroll. The club had already shed nearly half the $45 million player salary by 1996. The idea of milking the farm system appeared to make sense.

Appearances can be deceiving. The 1996 club did not yet boast enough premier young talent to commit to a youth movement. They finished a lowly tenth in the NL in runs scored despite three veterans enjoying career years. Among them were outfielders and newcomers Bernard Gilkey, who out of nowhere bashed 30 home runs and drove in 117 after his acquisition from St. Louis and set a franchise record with 44 doubles, and speedy free-agent signee Lance Johnson, who posted career-highs in hits (227), stolen bases (50), and batting average (.333) while slamming 21 triples, the most in the National League since 1930. That one-two-three punch also included catcher Todd Hundley, who exploded for 41

Todd Hundley helped bridge the gap at catcher for the Mets between the Gary Carter and Mike Piazza eras.
© JERRY COLI/DREAMSTIME

home runs and 112 RBI. But the only young farm-system contributor that shined was first baseman and flash-in-the-pan Butch Huskey.

That the Mets still struggled offensively proved an indictment of the farm system. But most disappointing was a trio nicknamed "Generation X" that included Isringhausen and fellow pitching prospects Paul Wilson and Bill Pulsipher. All three zoomed through the minors. Pulsipher debuted along with Isringhausen in 1995 and showed promise with a 5-7 record and 3.98 ERA. Considered by some the most talented of the threesome after being selected first overall in the 1994 amateur draft, Wilson earned a rotation spot the following spring.

The triumvirate was touted as the reincarnation of Seaver, Koosman, and Matlack. But the careers of Pulsipher and Wilson were derailed by injuries perhaps resulting from overuse in an era in which 120-pitch games were far more commonplace. The former struggled to find the plate, and the latter simply took beatings when he returned to the big leagues. Only Isringhausen thrived but not until arm injuries set him back as well and Oakland transformed him into a lights-out closer after the Mets dealt him in a disastrous 1999 trade.

Such failures resulted in regression. The 1996 Mets fell under .500 in early April and remained there despite flirting with the break-even mark into mid-July. A collapse thereafter cost Green his job. The club had lost four straight when McIlvaine pulled the plug, replacing Green with former Rangers manager Bobby Valentine, who was promoted from Triple-A Norfolk.

The hope was that the 46-year-old Valentine would extract more out of the young talent than Green, who had recently told reporters that Isringhausen and Wilson "don't belong in the big leagues." True or not, that was deemed no way to instill confidence. "That's a comment you should make behind closed doors," McIlvaine said. "When you're trying to develop players, a big part of that is building confidence. I'm not sure how much that builds their confidence when you criticize them like that."[2]

The Mets were not about to go out on a limb for Valentine, whom they only gave a two-year contract. Little could they have imagined he would guide them into their third era of greatness. The 1996 club was too far gone, but his impact proved undeniable the next season.

Valentine had arrived with a history and reputation for arrogance and volatility. During his tenure in Texas, he baited umpires and even opposing pitchers. He taunted Kansas City so intensely during one game in 1985 that Royals manager Dick Howser gave his pitchers the green light to throw beanballs—directly at him in the dugout. None accepted the "Valentine Challenge."

The perceived bitterness of the new Mets manager stemmed from a truncated playing career. Valentine showed tremendous potential after the Dodgers selected him fifth overall in the 1968 amateur draft. But a leg injury sustained in 1973 (after he'd been traded to the Angels) when his spike caught on the outfield wall robbed him of his speed and devastated his career. He considered himself better than any of the Dodger

Current manager Bobby Valentine (left) and former manager Joe Torre exchange pleasantries.
© JERRY COLI/DREAMSTIME

prospects he played with in the minors, including Ron Cey, Davey Lopes, and Steve Garvey. He never had a chance to prove it.

Valentine landed the job with Texas, which featured neither the hitting nor the pitching in most seasons to contend. They remained a middle-of-the-road team throughout his eight years at the helm. His firing in 1992 brought out the worst in him. He criticized the scouting staff and farm directors for what he believed was poor player development. "I'm a little arrogant, there's no doubt about that," Valentine admitted upon landing the job in New York after spending three seasons managing and mellowing in Japan. "I do get short when people try to tell me about things that I know about, and they're totally incorrect. I get insulted by that. But, yeah, maybe I've tried to temper it. I just got tired of fighting the battle."[3]

It was this tempered Valentine that took over the Mets. He had lessened his temper but not his passion for the game. He quickly strengthened his reputation as a tremendous motivator who gained respect from his players through studious preparation. After a slow start in 1997 that all but buried the Mets in a division race dominated by pitching-rich Atlanta, they hit their stride and joined the wild-card playoff battle. The Mets embarked on no long winning streaks—they simply performed consistently well. A four-game sweep of Pittsburgh in late June raised their record to 41-32, and another of Cincinnati a month later vaulted them to 56-42. A stretch of struggles in August and a five-game losing streak in September doomed the Mets to watching the postseason from home. But Valentine had turned the franchise around with an 88-74 finish.

He and new pitching coach Bob Apodaca, who arrived with him from Norfolk, had worked wonders. Among their triumphs was journeyman right-hander Rick Reed, who had bounced back and forth from Triple-A to the majors for four different organizations since 1988. Reed had worked with Valentine and Apodaca at Triple-A after signing with the Mets before the 1996 season.

Reed had angered fellow players a year earlier after accepting work from the Reds as a replacement player in spring training while his peers remained on strike. But he certainly proved himself worthy of a spot in the rotation after landing one in 1997 with the Mets. He emerged as the ace of the staff with pinpoint control and ability to keep hitters off-balance. He finished the season with a 13-9 record and fine 2.89 earned run average and remained a starting stalwart for the Mets into the next century.

Valentine quickly gained the admiration of his players. His reputation was no longer reality. "He might have done some things when he was younger," said Mets closer John Franco as his team inched to within four games of first place in late June. "But life is a learning process. He's been great."[4]

By that time, another change was about to alter the future of the franchise. McIlvaine was fired as general manager in July despite the sudden success of a club he had built, and he was replaced by 34-year-old assistant Steve Phillips. Co-owner Fred Wilpon provided him and the public an explanation perceived as rather half-baked given the generally positive results of McIlvaine's trades and free-agent signings. After all, it was the inability of the farm system to consistently produce major-league talent that had prevented the Mets from winning. And McIlvaine had dutifully canned Green when it was determined he was not extracting the most out of the young players. But Wilpon claimed McIlvaine was better suited for scouting. He was offered a position as a talent evaluator, but by 1998 he had accepted work as a special assistant for the Minnesota Twins.

Among the first orders of business for Phillips in the off-season was picking up where McIlvaine left off a year after the latter ripped off the Blue Jays in a trade for hitting-machine first baseman John Olerud, who proved himself back on track in 1997 after a poor year with Toronto. Olerud, who once threatened to become the first .400 hitter in major league baseball since Ted Williams in 1941, debuted with the Mets by batting .294 with 22 home runs, 102 RBI, and a .400 on-base percentage. Recognizing that Olerud still had plenty of baseball left in him at age 29, Phillips signed him to a three-year free-agent contract for $20 million. Olerud justified that faith by embarking on one of the finest displays of pure hitting in Mets history. He set franchise records with a .354 batting average and .447 on-base percentage in 1998.

The new GM continued to bolster the roster. He dealt promising minor-league pitcher A. J. Burnett to the Marlins, who were already rebuilding after winning a World Series, for established southpaw Al Leiter. And in May, he achieved the coup de grace, landing slugging catcher and future Hall of Famer Mike Piazza from Miami, which had acquired him a week earlier from the Dodgers. In exchange, the Mets dispatched immensely talented outfielder Preston Wilson, whose career would be marked on the bright side by tremendous displays of power, speed, and explosive seasons but on the flipside had a penchant for strike-outs and disappointing years. The deal angered incumbent starter Todd Hundley, whose absence due to injury had strapped the Mets at that position. He was moved to outfield upon his return, and then was dealt to the Dodgers in December.

The newcomers proved once again necessary for the well-being of the Mets, who beyond Alfonzo continued to fail to nurture top-level hitting or pitching talent. Though one could cite that the organization was in win-now mode and Wilson had been used to lure Piazza, it could also be argued that one or two premier additions from Norfolk could have meant the difference between a winner and a World Series contender.

The 106-win Braves precluded a battle for the division crown in 1998, but the Mets engaged in a lively scrap for the wild card. They just picked the wrong time to embark on a five-game losing streak. They owned a one-game lead on the Cubs for the playoff spot on September 20 before falling twice to miserable Montreal to drop into a tie with Chicago, one game ahead of surging San Francisco. Looming on the schedule was powerful Atlanta. Though the Braves had nothing to play for aside from heading into the postseason with momentum, they buried the Mets with a sweep.

A blowout defeat to end the season proved particularly galling. Losses by both the Cubs and Giants that day would have resulted in the Mets remaining alive in a three-way tie for the wild card had they won. Most frustrating was that Valentine chose veteran right-hander Armando Reynoso to start that game over early-season acquisition Hideo Nomo. The choice seemed logical on the surface—Reynoso had performed well down the stretch. But he was 0-6 lifetime against Atlanta with a bloated 6.37 ERA. And he got bombed out in the second inning that afternoon before Nomo arrived and hurled four shutout innings in his first major-

Shown here eyeing a popup, Mike Piazza was known more for his offense than his defense during a Hall of Fame career.

league relief appearance. By that time, however, the game was gone, and the Mets had punched their ticket home. Valentine bemoaned their misfortune in a gloomy clubhouse following the defeat. "I don't know what happened," he said. "If I knew, I would have done something about it. That's my frustration about it. Everything I tried didn't work. There should have been something."[5]

He would not find that something until 1999. But what he found that year and the next was something else.

CHAPTER FIFTEEN

Super Season

THE OLD BASEBALL CHESTNUT "YOU CAN'T TELL THE PLAYERS WITHOUT a scorecard" rang true for the 1999 Mets. The seeds were planted in December when they began the process of raising their payroll from $58 million to $71 million through trades and free agency.

The opening salvo in their battle for a National League championship was fired on the first day of that month when they signed premier third baseman Robin Ventura to a four-year, $32 million deal. General manager Steve Phillips viewed Ventura as a complete package—a consistent run producer with a high on-base percentage and five-time Gold Glove winner still in his prime at 32. Manager Bobby Valentine quickly learned that Ventura provided his club with positives beyond production. "It's hard to put into words. . . . He brings a real light-hearted perspective at times on the bench and in the clubhouse, and yet it's a hard-nosed perspective," Valentine explained.[1]

Phillips also pulled off a stunning trade the same day he signed Ventura that eventually ended John Franco's reign as a closer. The three-way swap with the Orioles and Dodgers sent Todd Hundley packing and brought fellow backup catcher Charles Johnson and outfielder Roger Cedeno to New York. But the star of the swap was closer Armando Benítez, who had clocked 102 miles per hour on his fastball. Though he had struggled in the playoffs, he was coming off a 54-save season for Baltimore and averaged well over a strikeout per inning every year. Benítez brought a dominating presence that Franco could not. Though Valentine claimed no intention to remove the aging Franco from the closer's role, the overpowering stuff of Benítez seemingly made that inevitable.

Then Phillips hit with a bombshell. He signed still-super and still-bizarre outfielder Rickey Henderson to a one-year contract with an option for the following season. While most major-league players—even the greatest—had either faded into mediocrity or long retired by age 40, Henderson remained one of the premier hitters and base thieves in the sport. Seven years after setting the all-time career stolen base record, he had led the American League with 66 swipes and 118 walks and scored 101 runs in 1998. Mets leadoff hitters batted just .237 with a .321 on-base percentage and 15 steals that year. The team stole fewer bags than did Henderson alone. Valentine understood the value if his team could receive anything close to the outrageous numbers Henderson had produced in his prime. "He was one of the most dominating players I managed against," he offered. "He might have lost a step, but he still has the ability to disrupt minds, as well as defenses."[2]

The transaction waters calmed well into spring training. Then Phillips scored again. He signed veteran right-hander Orel Hershiser to a one-year deal, then released fellow starting pitcher Hideo Nomo the next day. Hershiser had helped transform Cleveland into an American League champion following a stellar career with the Dodgers during which he established the all-time major-league record for consecutive scoreless innings and a reputation as a bulldog on the mound, especially in the postseason. Hershiser was 40 years old, and his prime had passed a decade earlier, but he remained a workhorse who could keep his team in games and certainly a positive clubhouse influence.

Phillips nailed it on all counts. Each major acquisition performed well in 1999 and made huge contributions to the playoff chase. Ventura hit behind Mike Piazza and prevented opposing hurlers from pitching around the stud slugger. The third baseman enjoyed his finest season with 32 home runs and career-highs in batting average (.301), doubles (38), and RBI (120). Cedeno came out of nowhere as a first-time starter in the big leagues to bat .313, score 90 runs, and steal 66 bases. Benítez had never been more dominant. He allowed just 40 hits in 78⅓ innings, struck out a career-best 128, and saved 22 games to permanently assume the closer spot. Henderson enjoyed a renaissance at the plate by hitting .315, his highest average since 1993, and remained feared by opposing pitchers, who issued 82 walks in helping him to a .423 on-base percentage. And Hershiser came as advertised with a 13-12 record and solid-in-the-steroid-era earned run average of 4.58.

Not that the Mets played like world-beaters from first pitch to last in the regular season. They opened on a 17-9 run then lost eight straight in early June to fall under .500 as the bats fell silent. Then they caught fire and remained red-hot into mid-September. The Mets went 65-30 during the bulk of the year, including a 17-1 victory in Houston on August 30 in which Alfonzo fashioned the greatest single-game performance in franchise history, smashing six hits, including three home runs, and scoring six runs.

The long hot streak allowed them to pull within one game of the first-place Braves (who else?) with a three-game series in Atlanta scheduled next. And in yet another case that proves the adage that good pitching beats good hitting, the Hall of Fame trio of John Smoltz, Greg Maddux, and Tom Glavine limited the Mets to six runs in a sweep that all but doomed the New Yorkers to a battle for the wild card. The reeling club then dropped three straight games in Philadelphia to convince many fans that they were destined to blow a playoff spot again.

The Mets headed into October a game-and-a-half behind Cincinnati. They could not afford another defeat as they prepared for a three-game set against Pittsburgh at Shea. And their pitchers rose to the occasion. July trade acquisitions Kenny Rogers, Rick Reed, and Hershiser performed brilliantly with help from Benítez and fellow reliever Pat Mahomes, who ran hot and cold but came up big with the season on the line. The sweep of the Pirates and good fortune as the Reds dropped two of three against the weak Brewers forced a one-game playoff in Cincinnati. And Al Leiter, who had performed far worse in 1999 than he had the previous year, handcuffed the Reds on two hits in a 5-0 triumph, his first complete game of the season. The victory featured home runs from Henderson and Alfonzo and landed the Mets in the playoffs for the first time in 11 years.

Franco was not the only Brooklynite who reveled in Leiter's accomplishment. Shortstop and July trade acquisition Shawon Dunston, who

Rick Reed posted a winning record in every season for the Mets.
© JERRY COLI/DREAMSTIME

hit .344 down the stretch in limited duty, harkened back to the effort of another Mets left-hander who had beaten Cincinnati in the 1973 NLCS. "Jerry Koosman, Jerry Koosman, Jerry Koosman!" Dunston repeated in celebration as the Mets began thinking about the Arizona Diamondbacks, their National League Division Series foe.[3]

That opponent boasted an advantage. Not only had they earned homefield advantage, but they had wrapped up their playoff spot weeks earlier and could set their rotation to open with scary-good southpaw Randy Johnson, who would soon be toting the second of his five Cy Young Award plaques. The Mets countered with far-less-talented Masato Yoshii. But they could take comfort in the knowledge that the right-hander had caught fire down the stretch with nine consecutive quality starts that lowered his ERA from 5.87 to 4.40.

Both arrived hot and cooled off quickly. With Valentine creating a righty-heavy lineup, the Mets battered Johnson early, but Yoshii could not hold the lead. Mets relievers Dennis Cook and Turk Wendell kept their team alive as the game reached the ninth inning tied at 4-4. That's

Lefty Al Leiter arrived from the Marlins to enjoy his finest seasons in the early 2000s.
© JERRY COLI/DREAMSTIME

when Alfonzo, who had homered off Johnson as the second batter in the game, played hero again. The Mets loaded the bases with one out against Johnson, who was removed in favor of Bobby Chouinard. He threatened to kill the rally by retiring Henderson, but Alfonzo took a mighty swing and smashed an upper-deck grand slam just inside the left-field foul pole to give his team a victory. "I didn't know if it was a foul or fair ball," said Alonzo. "I stayed at home plate, going, 'C'mon, c'mon.'"[4] The blow proved critical given that Arizona rebounded the next night to batter Rogers and even the series.

A throng of 56,180 packed Shea Stadium for Game 3, and they were rewarded. The Mets proved relentless despite no extra-base hits in a six-run sixth inning that featured RBI singles by Henderson, Olerud, Cedeno, and Darryl Hamilton. That placed them on the verge of an NLCS clash against Atlanta.

Some assumed they would first be required to overcome Johnson in Game 4. But Arizona manager Buck Showalter eschewed the temptation to pitch his ace on three days' rest and opted instead for sometimes-starter Brian Anderson. The lefty performed brilliantly, holding the Mets to just two runs in seven innings. The game could have been lost after Benítez allowed a two-run double in the seventh to turn a 2-1 lead into a 3-2 deficit. A single to left followed. But Valentine had shown the foresight to replace the weak-armed Henderson with Melvin Mora, who threw a strike to the plate to cut down the runner and prevent the Diamondbacks from taking a 4-2 lead.

Soon the stage was set for the unlikeliest of heroes to emerge. And that was backup catcher Todd Pratt, who had been forced into action when Piazza had been sidelined with a thumb injury. Pratt was hitless in four at-bats when he stepped to the plate in the tenth inning against Arizona reliever Matt Mantei with the score tied at 3-3 and unloaded a series-clinching blast to dead center to spark a celebration on the field and in the stands. "Oh, I wish you could see this!" imparted legendary Mets radio announcer Bob Murphy to his joyful listeners.

There had been much more to see in 1999. But the competition was destined to get even tougher, especially for a club that had lost nine of 12 games against Atlanta in both that season and the previous one. The Braves not only featured three Hall of Fame hurlers in Maddux, Glavine, and Smoltz. In an embarrassment of riches, 23-year-old right-hander Kevin Millwood had enjoyed a breakout season, compiling the excellent numbers that would periodically dot his career, and actually outperformed one and all among the terrific trio. The Mets boasted fine pitching. The Braves boasted the greatest staff in baseball.

It showed. Maddux, Millwood, and Glavine limited New York to just three earned runs in 21⅓ innings while controversial flash-in-the-pan closer John Rocker saved every game as Atlanta bolted to a 3-0 series lead. A sweep appeared likely when Reed, who was rolling along with a shut-out, surrendered successive home runs to Braves sluggers Brian Jordan and Ryan Klesko leading off the eighth inning in Game 4 to fall behind 2-1. But Olerud saved the season—at least temporarily—with a two-run single in the bottom half of the frame before Benítez closed it out.

The Mets had survived to live another day at Shea. But they were forced to overcome another poor performance by Yoshii, who, like a light switch, lost his groove after pitching three shutout innings. A lights-out effort by the relief corps kept Atlanta from scoring inning after inning with the season hanging in the balance. Hershiser offered a renaissance performance by blanking the Braves over three innings. Valentine nearly emptied his bullpen. And they all hurled shutout ball until a tiring Octavio Dotel allowed a run in the fifteenth. The Mets again were up against the wall blindfolded with the Braves ready and eager to pull the trigger. But they battled during every at-bat, working a single and three walks into a game-tying run before the slumping Ventura, who had been 1-for-18 in the series and was hampered by a bad knee, ended it by slamming a Kevin McGlinchy pitch over the wall in right-center for what would have been a grand slam had not a mob scene with his teammates prevented him from circling the bases and limited him to a single. Hope remained.

"It just seems like this team responds to dire situations," Ventura said. "We just play another day. It seems like we've been saying that for about a month and a half now. We can't lose another game. We're happy to just be playing."[5]

The craziness continued in Atlanta, where the Mets again refused to die despite a horrific outing by Leiter, who pitching on three days' rest for only the second time in his career, allowing the first seven batters he faced to reach base and put his team in a 5-0 crater with Millwood mowing down his mates. Mahomes, who battled control problems his entire career, came to the rescue with four scoreless innings, but the Mets still seemed doomed down 7-3 heading into the seventh. That's when the meat of the lineup battered Smoltz. Pinch-hitter Matt Franco doubled. Henderson doubled. Olerud singled. Piazza homered. Game tied.

The seesaw battle continued. A Mets bullpen that had risen to greatness time and again simply failed. Franco allowed a run in the eighth that knotted the score. Benítez blew a chance to send the series to a Game 7 by surrendering a run in the tenth. And Rogers, who had performed poorly throughout the playoffs, took his third postseason defeat by walking in the game-winner in the eleventh. What came as little surprise at that point—Rogers had by then allowed 20 earned runs in 19 career postseason innings—finally finished off the Mets in 1999. The left-hander would later pitch well for Detroit in its 2006 quest for a crown.

But that only served to frustrate Mets fans who wondered why he could not perform anywhere near that level for their team.

Few complained when Rogers, who had alienated some in Oakland and New York in 1999 with what they perceived as a disgruntled nature and aloof personality, signed a free-agent contract with Texas in the off-season. Meanwhile, Valentine looked forward to the 2000 season. First, however, he expressed his appreciation for what his team had accomplished. "I told my guys after the game that it might be a shorter winter or a longer winter for them but I think they played like champions," he said after the Game 6 defeat. "They should feel like champions. It's very difficult to come back from five runs and have a couple of leads. It's difficult to give it up, but we gave everything we had."[6]

Giving everything they had wasn't quite enough in 1999. It would not be in 2000 either. But the Mets would give themselves and their fans an even longer and more wonderful ride along the way.

CHAPTER SIXTEEN

The Subway Series

THE METS HAD SOME HOUSECLEANING TO DO BEFORE EMBARKING ON their 2000 season. Their defections and additions did not fill fans with optimism. Indeed, many believed their roster had been weakened since the loss to the Braves in the National League Championship Series.

The most significant blow was delivered by first baseman John Olerud, who hightailed it to hometown Seattle despite what he admitted being a significant offer from the Mets. His departure promised a drop in offensive production, defensive strength, and clubhouse stability. He was replaced by fellow free agent Todd Zeile, who, at 34, had remained a consistent run producer throughout his career. But he boasted neither the power nor the pure hitting prowess of Olerud and represented a significant downgrade defensively, especially considering the Mets planned to move him from third base to first, where he had only played sparingly in his career.

Then there were the thorny cases of malcontents Bobby Bonilla and Rickey Henderson, neither of whom were about to join the Bobby Valentine Fan Club. The pair had received significant criticism after reports surfaced that they spent the end of Game 6 of the 1999 NLCS playing cards in the clubhouse while their teammates battled on the field to keep their World Series hopes alive. Bonilla explained years later that Henderson had requested the card game to diffuse his anger at being removed from the action by Valentine.

That anger intensified in the off-season when general manager Steve Phillips refused to offer a two-year contract extension. The 41-year-old

Henderson had publicized his desire to be traded after it had become apparent that Valentine planned to provide some playing time in left field to Benny Agbayani, whom the manager believed at age 28 and having contributed to the playoff run the previous season deserved a chance. Henderson even threatened to skip the trip to Japan to open the regular season, though he did accompany the team for the series against the Cubs. He started both games as a leadoff hitter and managed just one hit while Agbayani played hero in the second game with the winning grand slam.

The problem was solved in early May when the Mets released Henderson, whose .207 batting average and five stolen bases certainly did not scream for everyday duty. The final straw fell when Mets fans booed him for a lack of hustle. He then shouted at a reporter the next day. Phillips tried to trade Henderson but found no takers. "After considering everything that happened last night and this morning, something had to be done," Phillips said. "I think the reasons are fairly obvious. No matter how much talent you have, if you continue to create problems and situations, you wear out your welcome. We got to the point where we had to compromise our ideals and what we expect from our players too often."[1]

Bonilla was long gone by then. The Mets traded for him before the 1999 season, and he quickly lost his starting job as his batting average dropped under .200. He spent most of the year as a pinch-hitter and received just four at-bats in the playoffs. He was released in early January by a team desperate to dump him without paying him the $6 million they owed outright. The club agreed to deferred money with an 8 percent annual interest rate on his salary that would not kick in until 2011. The result was payments of nearly $1.2 million every year until 2035. The contract that would continue to pay Bonilla until he was 72 years old became a running joke.

The result of such maneuvering in 2000 was an overhauled outfield that featured Agbayani, emerging prospect Jay Payton, and veteran Derek Bell, whom the Mets received from Houston along with starting pitcher Mike Hampton for outfielder Roger Cedeno and reliever Octavio Dotel in a trade that benefitted both teams. The club lost speed on the basepaths—they finished last in the National League in 2000 in stolen

Benny Agbayani became a fan favorite in 1999 and beyond.

bases—but gained power. The Olerud-for-Zeile swap cost the Mets runs that season as they fell to middle-of-the-pack offensively. But the addition of Hampton improved the rotation.

At least, it did eventually. Hampton and his starting mates suffered through a brutal start to the season—and it was not merely a reflection of the steroid era. Four poor outings in late April and early May raised his earned run average to a bloated 6.52. Reed managed just one quality start from April 27 into June. The staff allowed six runs or more in 14 of 20 games during one stretch in the early months but were often bailed out by the bats. The Mets averaged 7.4 runs per game in a nine-game April winning streak and continued to create fireworks through Independence Day.

The result, in a National League East in which the aging Braves had been downgraded from overpowering to merely great, was a race for the top. The Mets rotation finally found its groove and emerged as a force in July and beyond. The club surrendered three runs or less in all but two games during an 11-2 blitz that chopped their six-game deficit behind Atlanta in half. The Mets remained sizzling throughout August to forge a tie with the Braves.

A September swoon set them back but failed to knock them out of the race. They arrived in Atlanta for a three-game series on September 18 with a chance at first place with a sweep. And they figured they had the right man on the mound for the opener in Hampton, who had allowed just five runs in his previous 42 innings. But control issues that had plagued the southpaw early in the year returned against the Braves while mound opponent Greg Maddux performed as he had at his peak in a 6-0 shutout.

The task to keep the Mets alive in the division chase fell onto the shoulders of off-season trade-acquisition Glendon Rusch, who had proven himself a mildly pleasant surprise. But Rusch had been creamed the last time he faced Atlanta in early July when he allowed a season-high 13 hits in a blowout defeat. He had changed his approach in that game by throwing inside to back aggressive Brave hitters off the plate. The result was too many baseballs leaking over and yelling "hit me!" en route. Rusch vowed to maintain the game plan that had brought success.

It didn't work. He was knocked out in the second inning, and it was over. The Mets were not going to win their first division title since 1988, a drought that would continue until 2006. They had, however, clinched a second-straight wild card berth in a top-heavy National League that lacked depth.

Though the Mets arrived in the playoffs with momentum after winning their last five regular-season games, the good vibes turned bad when they not only lost Game 1 in San Francisco but also Bell as well due to a high ankle sprain. Benítez nearly placed his team in a 2-0 hole in the ninth inning the next night when he surrendered a three-run homer to J. T. Snow to blow a 4-1 lead. But he was bailed out by Jay Payton, who singled in the go-ahead run in the tenth, and Franco, who retired the Giants and dramatically fanned Bonds after Benítez yielded a single to open the bottom of the inning.

The Mets took the momentum and ran with it to Shea. Their knack for clutch play continued in Game 3 as their bullpen hurled eight scoreless innings—even Benítez rebounded by blanking San Francisco in the tenth and eleventh. A game-winning homer by Agbayani placed the Mets on the verge of a series triumph.

Valentine had a decision to make. Some believed he should start Rusch, who had faced two batters in Game 1, fanned both, and had not pitched since. But Valentine opted instead for Bobby Jones, whose ERA had soared over 5.00 the last two seasons and had become woefully inconsistent. The choice was widely criticized. One interested party who expressed faith in Jones was wife Kristi, hardly an impartial predictor, who guaranteed her husband would emerge with the victory. And Jones did better than that. He crafted the finest performance of his career—a one-hit shutout marred only by a Jeff Kent double in the fifth inning that broke up his perfect game.

The 4-0 victory that featured a two-run homer by Ventura catapulted the Mets into an NLCS showdown against St. Louis, which thankfully had eliminated Atlanta. It also motivated Leiter to praise his friend. "I'm so happy for Bobby Jones," he said. "I'm so proud of him. To go out and pitch the best game of his life and dismiss all the critics who thought it was a bad decision. He went out and nailed it."[2]

Now it was Hampton's turn to nail it. The lefty had motivation beyond helping the Mets continue their quest for a championship. And that was his impending free agency. Hampton and Phillips both expressed interest in negotiating a long-term contract to keep him in New York, but nothing had been accomplished, so the open market would soon beckon. He had performed well in the regular season but had done himself no favors with a poor performance in the NLDS opener that raised his career postseason earned run average to 5.85. And he had certainly taken a step back in 2000 after compiling an incredible 22-4 record in Houston the previous year. A rebound in the National League Championship Series would ensure a huge payday.

He rebounded like Bill Russell. What emerged as the Mike Hampton Series began in St. Louis with seven shutout innings in the opener in which a new hero emerged. And that was outfielder Timo Pérez, who had spent his career playing in Japan until the Mets signed him before the season. Valentine boldly used the September callup from Triple-A Norfolk to replace the injured Bell in the NLCS, and the move paid immediate dividends when Pérez doubled leading off the game and scored to give his team momentum they never lost in a 6-2 victory.

The Mets bore witness and benefitted from the puzzling and sudden breakdown of Cardinals right-hander Rick Ankiel the next night. His stunning loss of control that would soon kill his pitching career and force a permanent move to the outfield reared its ugly head in the first inning of Game 2 as he walked three batters, unloaded a wild pitch, and was removed. Payton eventually won the game with an RBI single, and the Mets had accomplished what few believed was possible. They had swept the Cardinals in St. Louis and returned to Shea with a clear shot at staying in New York for a Subway Series showdown against the Yankees.

The Cardinals had other ideas. They pounded Reed in Game 3 for an 8-2 victory and bolted ahead 2-0 the next night. That is when the Mets auditioned for what could have been a Doublemint Gum commercial. They set a League Championship Series record with five doubles in the first inning against tough St. Louis southpaw Darryl Kile. Pérez, Alfonzo, Piazza, Ventura, and Agbayani all slammed two-baggers to give their team a lead they would not relinquish despite a shaky performance on the mound by Jones.

One could hardly have imagined Hampton following his Game 1 masterpiece with an even better effort to clinch the series. But he indeed embarked on one of the finest performances in playoff history. He faced no more than four batters in any inning for a 7-0 complete-game shutout sparked again by Pérez with a single, stolen base, and run in a three-run first. The frustrated Cardinals came unglued, which might explain an ugly incident that marred the event in the eighth when pitcher Dave Veres hit Payton in the eye with a fastball. The Mets outfielder began charging the mound as both benches and bullpens cleared, but he was restrained by Agbayani and Valentine. The Cardinals were booed lustily by the sellout crowd, who delighted in chanting the lyrics from the iconic 1969 rock hit *Na Na Hey Hey Kiss Him Goodbye*. Their team soon added revenge to their list of achievements by polishing off their foe, 7-0.

In a surprise akin to the Earth orbiting the sun, Hampton was voted Most Valuable Player in the series. Far more significant was that the Mets were headed to the World Series for the first time since 1986. Upon clinching the NL crown, the players took a victory lap around Shea Stadium, then headed to the clubhouse for a celebration that returned to the field as Pratt sprayed the fans with champagne. Soon, Hampton was talking about the challenge to come as his teammates expressed a hope that the Yankees would indeed emerge from the American League Championship Series against Seattle. "We're four wins away from fulfilling that fantasy," he declared.[3]

Those four wins would indeed have to be earned against the two-time defending World Series champions and crosstown rivals. But the Yankees appeared far more vulnerable than they had in 1998 and 1999 when they averaged 106 victories and swept both San Diego and Atlanta in the Fall Classic. The Bronx Bombers lost 15 of their last 20 regular season games to finish 87-74 and barely snuck by the Athletics and Mariners in the playoffs. They boasted a barely-above-average attack for a steroid-era club and nary a starter with an earned run average lower than 3.70 despite the presence of superstars Roger Clemens and Andy Pettitte in the rotation. Even greatest-closer-of-all-time Mariano Rivera was coming off a down year. Many considered the Mets a more talented club. And they had plenty of motivation beyond winning it all. They resented being considered "second fiddle" in the Big Apple.

Among those that believed the Yankees boasted no advantage from their World Series experience (only four Mets had played in one, and Al Leiter was the only starting player among them) was backup outfielder Darryl Hamilton. He offered that the Subway Series was a completely different animal to which the Bronx Bombers would also be forced to adjust. "This is something totally new," he said. "It's going to be crazy. One out is important in a playoff game. Tomorrow night, one pitch and people are going to be screaming. I don't think all the experience in the world is going to prepare you for what's going to happen in the next 10 days."[4]

Agbayani did his team no favors by predicting on the Howard Stern radio show that the Mets would bury the Bombers in five games. Though some interpreted his words as merely a joke, former Mets and current Yankees pitcher David Cone knew first-hand that providing bulletin-board material that could incentivize an opponent is never a good idea. He had done just that in his short-lived stint as a newspaper columnist during the 1988 playoffs. "You see how naïve some guys are," Cone said. "They make an innocent mistake and all of a sudden it's on the front page and they are reeling."[5]

Hamilton was right about one thing: The Subway Series was limited to just five games. One could only speculate as to how it would have unfolded had the inconsistent Benítez not blown a 3-2 ninth-inning lead in the opener at Yankee Stadium. Setting a tone for a series in which the only major statistical difference proved to be the Mets walking 25 batters to just 10 for Yankees pitchers, Benítez ruined a fine performance by Leiter by allowing a walk to score the tying run. Turk Wendell then surrendered the game-winner in the twelfth.

Game 2 featured more fireworks, greatly revolving around Yankees starter Roger Clemens, whose temper got the best of him in the first inning. The seeds of his angry and unprovoked outburst were planted in July when he nailed Piazza in the head with a pitch. The volatile right-hander was roundly criticized for the incident but seemed unaffected, even vindictive, when he nearly plunked Seattle superstar Alex Rodriguez on successive pitches in the American League Championship Series. Yet the Mets catcher suspected Clemens would be on his best behavior in the World Series.

He wasted no time proving otherwise. The ultracompetitive pitcher was out of control by the first inning. Some have claimed his inexplicable anger was exacerbated by "roid rage" despite Clemens never having been proven guilty of steroid use. Whatever the motivation, he simply lost it after fielding a sawed-off piece of Piazza's bat on a foul ball in the first inning. Clemens dangerously fired its jagged edge toward Piazza, who had begun running to first base unsuspecting that he had not hit it fair. Piazza took a step toward the mound, bat handle in hand. "What's your problem? What the fuck is your problem?" Piazza snapped.[6]

Clemens claimed strangely to umpire Charlie Reliford that he thought he was throwing a ball, not a bat. Why then, wondered Piazza, did he fire it at him and not to first base? The verbal confrontation never escalated into a physical one because Piazza remained level-headed in an atmosphere of extreme tension as the sellout crowd screamed in anticipation of a fight. His initial temptation was to plant his fist on Clemens' face. He had been prepared for just such a circumstance working with friend and karate expert John Bruno. But Piazza also worried that the burly Clemens would kick his butt. And he understood that getting ejected in a World Series game the Mets desperately needed to win would be viewed as selfish. So, he returned to the batter's box.

Piazza also wrote the following about his motivation in a 2013 book he co-authored with Lonnie Wheeler:

> There was something else holding me back, as well. Leading up to this night, there had been so much public clamoring to see Clemens and me go mano-a-mano, such a loathsome display of bloodlust, that I wanted no part of it for that very reason. It had evolved into a gladiator mentality. It's my job to feed the mob? I have to run out and fight Roger Clemens because the fans expect me to? I had no interest in being the people's puppet. Never did. The whole atmosphere just sucked the steam out of me.[7]

Some in the media and even among his teammates, including Hamilton and Hampton, criticized Piazza for what they perceived as chickening out. Among the former was *New York Post* sports columnist Wallace Mathews, who lambasted the Mets star.

"Piazza's move toward Clemens was half-hearted and, in a way, kind of laughable," Mathews wrote. "He is supposed to be one of the leaders of this team and considering his anemia at the plate . . . he probably could have made no greater contribution to his team last night than to take a real run at Clemens and try to get him out of the game. It's not sportsmanship, but it is gamesmanship of the same kind Clemens and the Yankees played on them. And the way things turned out, given a second chance the Mets would make that Piazza-for-Clemens trade in a heartbeat if they could."[8]

Indeed, Clemens remained locked in and mowed down the Mets on just two hits through eight shutout innings. The visitors kicked up their heels for five runs to chop their deficit to 6-5 in a stirring ninth-inning rally that included a Piazza homer and three-run bomb by Payton off none other than Rivera. But they finally succumbed and were forced to return to Shea down 2-0 in the series.

A fine performance by Reed and the bullpen in a Game 3 win provided hope, but the Mets simply did not hit well enough to topple the Yankees, particularly with runners on base. Threats fizzled out inning after inning to waste solid pitching. The Mets were blanked after a Piazza home run in Game 4.

Valentine then made what some criticized as a tactical error in the series ending defeat. He bypassed his bullpen to allow Leiter to pitch the ninth in a 2-2 tie. His confidence appeared well-served when the ace fanned the dangerous duo of Tino Martinez and Paul O'Neill to start the inning. But Valentine refused to summon Franco after a walk and single raised the left-hander's pitch count to a ridiculous 141. Light-hitting Luis Sojo then singled in the go-ahead run, with another scoring on a throwing error. Sojo was pleasantly surprised that the weary Leiter bypassed his nasty slider in favor of a get-me-over heater. "It was like a [batting practice] fastball," Sojo said.[9]

Rivera soon polished off the Mets, retiring Piazza on a deep drive to center, and Shea fell silent aside from a few hundred Yankee-fan revelers. But the Mets felt no shame. They had battled their American League rival tooth-and-nail in every game. Wendell offered that had the defeats been blowouts, "I'd be like, geez, how did we get here? But all these games could have gone either way. They could have swept us in four. We could have swept them in four. We get a break, and it's a totally different situation. It's just unfortunate we didn't capitalize on some things."[10]

If they had, what followed would not have been so painful. Players that reach the World Series must win them because they never know if their teams will earn another opportunity. There would be no more chances for Valentine as Mets manager. Or, for that matter, for the Mets until the second decade of the new millennium.

CHAPTER SEVENTEEN

The End of Valentine's Day—And Howe

PERHAPS FOR SOME, IT WAS AGE KICKING IN. FOR OTHERS, IT WAS JUST A slump. For a few, it marked the start of a career slide. But whatever it was, it affected nearly every hitter on the 2001 Mets roster. And it resulted in the feeblest offense in the National League.

The club scored 165 fewer runs than they had their previous season. Edgardo Alfonzo experienced the most pronounced collapse, falling from a 2000 slash line of .324/25/94 to .243/17/49. But he had plenty of company. Mike Piazza lost 18 runs batted in. Todd Zeile dropped from 22 home runs to 10. Robin Ventura's RBI total fell from 84 to 61. Jay Payton's home run and RBI production was cut nearly in half. And even sparkplug Darryl Hamilton's batting average fell 62 points, motivating his release in mid-July.

Such impotence ruined another fine year from the rotation, particularly Rick Reed, Al Leiter, and right-handed free-agent addition Kevin Appier, all of whom posted ERAs under 4.00 at the height of the steroid era. The staff allowed the fewest walks in the National League—a critical benefit given the number of home runs flying out of major-league ballparks.

Not that the 2001 Mets merely withered and died. They withered, died, and resurrected. Remarkably, considering they were coming off a pennant year, they failed to even win three straight games until mid-June. A seven-game losing streak in July lowered their record to 54-68 and plunged them 13½ games out of first place. They were presumed dead until a shocking 25-6 run in which their bats finally began booming in September. The Mets catapulted to within three games of the lead, but that proved to be a classic case of too little, too late. Two defeats in Atlanta followed, and they were cooked.

Their plight meant nothing in comparison to the horror felt by fans and all New Yorkers—especially the families of those who perished—after terrorists guided planes into the Twin Towers and killed thousands on September 11. Manager Bobby Valentine and his players visibly and selflessly visited rescue and recovery workers at Ground Zero digging bodies out of the rubble. They helped bring a sense of camaraderie and togetherness to the community. "When we went down there for the first time, you could smell it," Valentine said. "You could still feel it. You could see the filth on the faces of the workers. When they saw us, their faces lit up. You could see their teeth through their black masks."[1]

The return of baseball to Shea Stadium and other ballparks around the country helped bring America back to life. The Mets donated about $500,000—their day's pay—on September 21 to a rescue fund for the families of firefighters and police officers killed in the attacks. That date marked their first game since 9/11 and featured uplifting songs performed by such stars as Diana Ross and Liza Minnelli. And Piazza buoyed the spirits of Mets fans further when he smashed a home run in the eighth inning to give them a 3-2 victory over an Atlanta team against whom they were making a belated run for the division crown.

"I'm just so happy I gave the people something to cheer," Piazza said. "There was a lot of emotion. It was just a surreal sort of energy out there. I'm just so proud to be a part of it tonight. These people are great. New York has been so strong through all this. I feel so sad. I met two kids today who lost their fathers."[2]

The city bounced back. The Mets did not. General manager Steve Phillips engineered a flurry of trades for aging veterans in the off-season, sending away Robin Ventura, Glendon Rusch, Todd Zeile, and Appier in the process. None of the departed proved impactful to their new teams, but neither did the additions to the Mets, such as second baseman Roberto Alomar, first baseman Mo Vaughn, and right fielder Jeromy Burnitz.

All three former stars were at least 33 years old and fading fast. Alomar ended his 12-year run as an All-Star in his first year with New York.

Vaughn had lost his entire 2001 season to a ruptured tendon in his left arm, ending a run as a perennial RBI machine, and would never be the same. Burnitz proved far more puzzling. He had averaged more than 100 runs batted in over the previous five seasons in Milwaukee. His production plummeted with the Mets. Burnitz posted career-worsts with a .215 batting average, 19 home runs, and 54 RBI in 2002. The trio that was supposed to create punch to what had been a punchless lineup in 2001 averaged just 19 homers and a shocking 60 RBI in their first campaigns with their new team. That was not what Phillips had in mind considering the Mets' 2002 Opening Day payroll hovered at $94.6 million, which ranked sixth in Major League Baseball.

What he also did not have in mind was a terrible year. The surprisingly weak lineup prevented ace Al Leiter from compiling a better record than 13-13, and the rest of the rotation, including newcomers Pedro

Mo Vaughn concluded his brilliant career with the Mets in 2002 and 2003.
© JERRY COLI/DREAMSTIME

Astacio, Shawn Estes, and Steve Trachsel (who had arrived in 2001), failed to perform to expectations.

Even a deep and effective bullpen could not save the 2002 Mets, who took advantage of a weak division to surge into first place in May before falling out of the race. A 6-23 stretch in August and September included the longest home losing streak ever for the franchise, a mean feat given the ineptitude of the 1962 club and beyond. The skein reached 15 with a loss to Florida on September 2, marking the longest in National League history. "It is demoralizing," said Piazza after their fourteenth consecutive defeat at Shea. "Everyone has had losing streaks, everyone has had slumps. But this is uncharted waters for me. I'm a little bit in shock."[3]

The Mets rebounded to win seven in a row but collapsed to finish the year. By that time, Valentine was destined for dismissal. One losing season after five winning ones had cost him his job. He had met with owner Fred Wilpon and expressed his desire for a greater role in personnel decisions in 2003, the final year of his deal. Silence. Valentine then asked about the renewal of contracts for his coaches. Crickets. Soon Wilpon lowered the boom. He told Valentine it had been a difficult decision but that he believed the Mets had underachieved considering the talent Phillips had acquired. Wilpon questioned his performance as a motivator of veteran players. He felt any club featuring the talents of Piazza, Vaughn, Alomar, Alfonzo, Burnitz, Leiter, and Benítez should not finish in the cellar. "We put very good players in place who didn't play very well," Wilpon complained. "It's best to jump-start and get a manager to motivate these players and get the best out of the veterans and the young players."[4]

Valentine certainly had an inkling his firing was possible. Wilpon had urged him with a month left in the season to "play every game like it's the World Series," and then the losses continued to pile up. And when Wilpon countered Valentine's request for more input on personnel decision by responding that he did not operate that way, the manager retorted, "Maybe you should." If that was not the final straw, it was certainly among the last.[5]

Valentine had often disagreed with Phillips and Wilpon on personnel decisions. Asking for more power was his way of refusing to go out with a whimper. "I'd like to think that probably my undoing was I had to be me," he said. "When I was in those meetings the last seven years, I nodded. I finally decided not to nod anymore."[6]

In one of the ironies of Mets history, Wilpon replaced a manager whose team had experienced the longest home losing streak in National League history with one coming off a year in which he guided his club to the longest winning streak in American League history. And that was Art Howe, who was released from his contract with Oakland to join the Mets. Howe had stunningly guided the rebuilding Athletics to 20 consecutive victories in a stunning playoff run in 2002. The season of dreams in which general manager Billy Beane embraced the newfangled philosophy of analytics to build his roster inspired the book and the movie *Moneyball* starring Brad Pitt. The penny-pinching A's could not afford to keep Howe after he finished second in the AL Manager of the Year balloting. But the Mets could—he signed a four-year contract for $9.4 million.

Not that Howe was their first choice. They lost out to Tampa Bay on Lou Piniella and the Chicago Cubs on Dusty Baker. But Howe was not complaining about playing third fiddle in the managerial search. "I might not be the first choice, but I'm the right choice," he said.[7]

Not if 2003 was any indication. But then, what transpired was not all his fault. Lady Luck and Father Time conspired to prevent Howe from employing the same level of talent Wilpon claimed Valentine had mismanaged. Age and injuries that had been taking a toll on the veterans overcame them that season.

The first to fall was Vaughn, who never played again after sidelining himself on May 2 with lingering knee pain that caused him to announce his retirement after the season.

The news was little better for Piazza, who suffered a strained right groin while backing away from a pitch on May 16 and left the park in a wheelchair. A muscle had torn away from his bone, leading to a four-month absence. He had already been struggling with nagging injuries and the unpalatable attempts by the Mets to move him from catcher to first base. His departure in the midst of a tear that had raised his average to .336 devastated a club desperate for hitting. The lineup had become a shell of what had been intended.

So had a patchwork pitching staff. The Mets had signed 37-year-old future Hall of Fame left-hander Tom Glavine to bolster the rotation, but the ravages of age had seemingly taken hold of him as well. Coming off a typically fine year for Atlanta, he suffered his worst year. His victory total fell from 18 to nine, and his ERA soared from 2.96 to 4.52. Glavine rebounded to perform well for New York into his forties, but his performance in 2003 contributed to a terrible season at Shea.

The Mets opened the season with the biggest payroll in the National League but quickly shed salary after losing Vaughn and Piazza and falling 12 games out of first place in mid-May. They traded the struggling and all-but-cooked Alomar to the White Sox for three prospects. Soon Burnitz and Benítez were gone to the Dodgers and Yankees, respectively, in similar deals. The trades netted nine players, none of whom brought anything of value but cost savings to the Mets. The purge sent the club reeling further in 2003. Stretches of 11-29 and 1-16 doomed the club to a 66-95 record, their worst in a decade.

The housecleaning had claimed one other significant victim. And that was Phillips, who was dismissed in mid-June and replaced by assistant Jim Duquette. A perception grew with each defeat that Phillips had done the franchise a disservice by focusing on filling the roster with aging veterans while the farm system continued its failure to stock the major-league club with talent. Wilpon, whose son Jeff had assumed more responsibility and disagreed with the Phillips philosophy, voiced that displeasure following the firing.

"We will attempt to energize this team this year and in future years by getting younger and more athletic," said the elderly owner. "We will strive to create a healthy mix of young and veteran players. Our minor-league system will be essential to our ability to be successful now and in the future."[8]

Wilpon considered Duquette the ideal successor. He had toiled in the Mets' minor-league and scouting departments for five years before taking over the Astros' farm system in 1997. He returned to serve as the player personnel director before accepting the job of Phillips' assistant before the 1999 season. His experience building from the ground up intrigued Wilpon and led to his promotion.

Duquette struck out in his return for Vaughn, Burnitz, and Benítez. The Mets had, however, launched a bit of a youth movement by elevating premier shortstop prospect José Reyes, who hit his stride a month later and continued to sizzle. He raised his average from .200 to .316 in a seven-week stretch that included a 17-game hitting streak during which he scored 18 runs and stole seven bases. The Mets also tied hope to such prospects as versatile infielder Ty Wigginton and catcher-first baseman Jason Phillips. They would have welcomed opportunities to send ready-and-waiting pitching standouts to the Shea Stadium mound as well, but the cupboard was bare.

The result was imbalance in playing out the new philosophy, which produced negative results for Howe in 2004 as well. The average age of the top three starters—Leiter, Glavine, and Steve Trachsel—was 36. The bullpen boasted no young standouts. Reyes lost most of his season to a back injury. The lineup remained one of the weakest in baseball. Howe kept his team around .500 and in the race in a weak division into July before fading. And when the Mets collapsed, they took it to an extreme. They lost 19 of 21 games in August and September to finish the season 71-91. By that time, Howe had already been informed of his termination.

Duquette was soon to follow. He was forced out as GM at the end of the year and replaced by former Mets senior assistant general manager Omar Minaya, who had earned the distinction the past three seasons in Montreal as the first Hispanic general manager in major-league history. Duquette would hang around as senior vice president of baseball operations under Minaya, who signed a five-year contract. Wilpon cited "special skills as a talent evaluator" for hiring Minaya and stressed the move was more an embracing of that talent than an indictment of Duquette.

The new GM spoke about maintaining what he perceived as Duquette's plan of building a team around pitching, defense, and athleticism despite the fact that the 2004 club featured an aging, mediocre pitching staff, ranked second last in the National League defensively, and was only moderately athletic. "They have a plan here and I want to work with that plan, because at the end of the day I want to win," Minaya said. "It's the dream of this New York kid to win a World Series here and have a parade down Broadway. That's my dream."

The 57-year-old Howe, who would not manage again in the majors, had gained a reputation as well-liked by his players but a poor tactician, which is a deadly drawback in the National League, where managers cannot benefit from designated hitters limiting pinch-hitting and pitching-change decisions. Wilpon admitted to erring by hiring Howe, stating that the results spoke for themselves. But injuries, age, and a lack of youthful talent hamstrung Howe. Given the circumstances, he had no chance to win.

Among those mentioned as possible replacements were former Mets standouts Gary Carter, Lenny Dykstra, and Wally Backman, as well as veteran managers such as Lou Piniella, Buck Showalter, and Bob Brenly. Even Valentine was rumored to be returning. But Minaya threw a curve by hiring ex-Yankees standout Willie Randolph as the first African-American manager in franchise history.

Randolph had been serving as that team's coach since 1994 with the hope of landing a managerial job. He continued to be passed over despite interviews with several clubs, including the Mets when he failed to impress Phillips, who hired Howe instead. That made it even sweeter when he was informed that he had been offered not only his first job as manager, but it would also allow him to stay in New York. The cherry on top was that Randolph grew up a Mets fan from the team's inception after his family moved to Brooklyn when he was an infant. "I think my wife had to pull me off the ceiling, I was so excited," he said about his reaction to the wonderful news. "It's a lot of emotion running through your body, the fact that you finally get your opportunity, you're doing it in your hometown, for the team you rooted for as a kid."[9]

Randolph was fortunate in another way. He was given the opportunity to manage arguably the greatest all-around homegrown position player in franchise history.

CHAPTER EIGHTEEN

It's All Wright

A THEME RUNNING THROUGH METS HISTORY WELL INTO THE NEW century has been success kick-started not by forking out big bucks to free agents but through the infusion of young talent. The influx of such superstars as Tom Seaver and Jerry Koosman in the sixties and Darryl Strawberry and Dwight Gooden in the eighties launched eras highlighted by the only two World Series championships in franchise history.

The inability of the club to consistently produce premier players from its farm system remained a drawback for decades. But one quite impactful exception emerged in the early 2000s. And that was third baseman David Wright, a late first-round draft pick in 2001 who rocketed through the farm system to make his major-league debut three years later. Unlike many young Mets of the past who did not shine as brightly or burned out quickly, the superstar third baseman did everything well. He hit for average and power, stole bases, covered ground defensively, and even flashed a Gold Glove. His good looks, engaging personality, and charitable work provided an added attraction for fans.

Wright was born five days before Christmas in 1982, the son of a Norfolk, Virginia, police officer who valued discipline in his parenting after following the plight of too many misguided youths as part of his job. Young David embraced the same values and helped his parents raise three younger brothers against whom he eventually competed heatedly in a variety of athletic endeavors only when their homework and household chores had been completed. Prioritizing academics resulted in Wright maintaining an A average at Hickory High School, where the only dis-

David Wright emerged as one of the most popular and productive Mets ever but could not overcome the injuries that shortened his career.

play of unruliness was a thrown hamburger in the cafeteria in response to a french fry tossed in his direction.

Wright had long before that developed a passion for baseball. He begged his grandfather to partake in a game of Wiffle ball or his father to play catch in the backyard as a small child. Despite being just three years old, he recalled the jubilant reaction of his father when the Mets won the 1986 World Series. His dad had embraced the Mets as his team because their Triple-A club played in nearby Norfolk. And David rooted right along with him.

The younger Wright spent hours at age six and beyond slamming balls off a tee. So advanced had he become as a player that by age nine, he had earned a spot in a league for older kids. His father coached the club but refused to give his son any breaks. He placed David in the detested position of right field when the boy vastly preferred to play shortstop. Wright eventually dominated the local little-league ranks. Among the coaches that took notice was Allan Erbe, who doubled as a Chicago Cubs scout. He made the bold prediction to fellow scouts that the 11-year-old would someday compete in the big leagues. "No doubt in my mind," Erbe later recalled. "It was a combination of my experience and intuition. But aside from that, he was head and shoulders above every other kid."[1]

Wright played shortstop and third base at Hickory. He was named all-state after a junior season in which he batted .507 and was ranked among the top 40 senior prospects in the country by *Baseball Digest*. He soon committed to Georgia Tech, which needed a replacement at third base for eventual Yankees star Mark Teixeira. Yellow Jackets baseball coach Danny Hall crowed that he had just signed the premier high school third baseman in the country, but he was in for a disappointment when Wright hit .538 as a senior, was named Gatorade Virginia Player of the Year to elevate his stock, and was selected by his beloved Mets in the draft. Soon he was receiving a $960,000 signing bonus to start his professional career.

Unlike other 18-year-olds fresh out of high school who dip their toes in the water and are overwhelmed by such a challenge until gaining their confidence, Wright immediately established the consistent production that marked his career until injuries derailed what seemed destined to end with enshrinement in the Hall of Fame. He batted .300 with nine stolen bases in just 36 games at the Rookie League level before embarking on a steady and seemingly inevitable ascension to The Show. His performance in Class-A and Class-A Advanced the next two seasons proved nearly identical—40 stolen bases and 168 RBI combined with a tremendous eye and patience, resulting in a .369 on-base percentage. It was as if the discipline instilled upon him by his parents carried over to his mindset in the batter's box.

Wright was merely warming up. He managed one of the greatest minor-league seasons in franchise history in 2004, batting .363 with an even more absurd .467 on-base percentage at Double-A Binghamton to earn a promotion to Triple-A. He not only bashed baseballs but won over the hearts and minds of baseball fans and the organization. On Memorial Day weekend that year, he stayed throughout an auction in which his valuable jersey was to be sold and even told bidders he would take the winner to lunch, thereby driving up the price for charity.

His callup to the Mets was merely a matter of time. An injury to Mike Piazza, who had been switched from catcher to first base, necessitated Ty Wigginton moving from third to first and resulted in Wright making his heralded Mets debut on July 21. Wright struggled mightily out of the gate, heated up with a six-RBI game in Milwaukee, then cooled off in St. Louis. Concerned that he might be overwhelmed by the challenge of performing amid great fanfare in a major market, the club arranged a meeting between Wright and Cardinals star third baseman Scott Rolen, who certainly overcame such obstacles in Philadelphia by winning National League Rookie of the Year honors in 1997 before blossoming into one of the premier players in the sport. Rolen, like Wright, was only 21 when he arrived in the big leagues. "He told me not to get caught up in the expectations," Wright said. "A lot of expectations will be put on you but you can't put them on yourself."[2]

Wright was also getting help from Mets utility player Joe McEwing, who took him under his wing as a pet project, and Piazza, who provided advice only a grizzled veteran could give. The pressure of playing in the majors, as well as facing pitchers with superior control, had caused Wright to lose his discipline at the plate. He managed just two walks in

Established standout third baseman Scott Rolen proved quite the teacher in helping David Wright soar to stardom.
WIKIMEDIA COMMONS

his first 72 plate appearances as his on-base percentage fell to .265 on August 8. An overeager Wright in one game grounded out on the first pitch with two runners in scoring position. "When I came back to the dugout, Piazza came over to me and put his arm around my shoulder," Wright recalled. "He said, 'Relax.' He said the pitcher was in trouble, not me, and that I swung at the pitch he wanted me to swing at, a slider low and away. Mike said: 'He had to throw strikes in that situation, and you could have waited to get your pitch. You didn't have to expand your strike zone.'"[3]

Wright also benefitted from a meeting with manager Art Howe, who assured him that the Mets were satisfied with his progress and that the hits would start falling in. And they did. Wright sizzled in a road trip to Colorado and San Francisco with 12 hits in six games to raise his average from .261 to .302. He remained consistently productive for the rest of the year. And though he finished with just 14 walks, he emerged quickly as the best all-around player on the team in the primo three spot in the lineup, and the patience at the plate that had been so pronounced in the minors returned in 2005.

He also displayed greater power as his rookie season progressed. At one point, teammate Vance Wilson suggested to Wright that he should become more aggressive at the plate because he was hitting too many weak singles. He smashed a 455-foot homer in his next at-bat, then shot a glance into the dugout and winked at Wilson as he rounded third base.

Wright just kept right on raking year after year. The old "sophomore slump" disease that had devastated ballplayers for generations did not infect Wright, who achieved in 2005 perhaps the greatest season for a second-year player in Mets history. He won the team Triple Crown by batting .306 with 27 home runs and 102 RBI. His 42 doubles were the franchise's second-highest single-season total ever (behind Bernard Gilkey's 44 in 1996).

His performance combined with that of emerging standout and triples machine José Reyes to offer rare optimism about the long-term future of the Mets. Reyes emerged as a force when he too increased his walk total and on-base percentage to take advantage of his speed. Wright made a habit from 2005 forward of driving home Reyes, who averaged 106 runs scored over the six healthy seasons he played.

Defensive proficiency came less naturally for Wright, whose hands and wrists as a hitter were quicker than his feet in the field. He struggled at third base until the second half of 2005 when he showed off his glove with a play some viewed as the best that season in Major League Base-ball. In the seventh inning of an early August game against San Diego, he robbed Brian Giles of a hit by sprinting after a flare down the left-field line and snagging the ball *barehanded* in his fingertips with full extension. Longtime MLB highlight show *This Week in Baseball* indeed selected it as its Play of the Year.

In the process of making life miserable for opponents, Wright was ingratiating himself to Mets fans. Young women and teenage girls swooned over his athleticism and movie-star good looks. Some shouted out marriage proposals before games. Soon they were wearing shirts that

Triples machine José Reyes led the National League four times in that department as a member of the Mets.

read "MRS. WRIGHT." Meanwhile, one and all appreciated that he preferred to stay grounded, not an easy task given the temptations of starring in New York City. He remained careful about those with whom he associated. And he refused to allow fame and fortune to lure him away from the old friends he valued. He launched the David Wright Foundation to battle multiple sclerosis. He even understood when the Mets renewed his contract at the major-league minimum following the 2005 season rather than offer the lucrative extension that he needed to maintain a positive attitude about his life and career.

"I did not agree, but that's life," he said. "I make a lot more money than both my parents combined, so, in my mind, I've got it pretty good. How many other 23-year-olds get to play a game for a living and act like a kid? The worst day on a ball field is better than the best day in any office. I refuse to have a bitter taste in my mouth about the game. As soon as baseball becomes a job, as soon as I stop caring, as soon as the smile goes away, I'll hang up my spikes and do something else."[4]

Injuries would force that day upon Wright far sooner than he anticipated, but he certainly had plenty of great baseball left in him. He signed endorsement deals, appeared on *The Late Show with David Letterman*, and even accepted a dinner invitation to the White House. But when the games began, he was focused. Such was certainly the case in 2006 when he made darn sure he would not again be passed over for the NL All-Star team. Wright sizzled from the start with an eight-game hitting streak that featured three home runs and 12 RBI. His torrid hitting helped set the stage for wire-to-wire dominance by the Mets in the NL East. He maintained a .300-plus batting average for all but three days into late August, then finished the year on a 12-game tear to finish with a slash line of .311/26/116. He earned NL Player of the Month honors in June and placed ninth in the Most Valuable Player voting. He also became the first player in major-league history to slug a home run in his first All-Star Game at-bat.

Wright had to wait no longer for the megadeal he had earned. He signed a six-year, $55 million contract that August that he believed planted the seeds that would enable him to remain with the team he embraced as a kid throughout his career. "I have wanted to be a lifelong

Met and this is the first step in that direction," he said. "It's a special feeling to be drafted by my favorite team. To know I'm going to be a Met for the next six or seven years is going to be special."[5]

One might have feared the pressure of playing up to the contract would have negatively affected Wright—and perhaps it did in a 2006 National League Championship Series defeat in which he managed just four hits in seven games. But Wright raked in a sweep of the Dodgers to help land his team in the NLCS and continued to strengthen his reputation as one of the most productive all-around offensive players in the sport while emerging as a Gold Glove third baseman.

Wright toiled endlessly on all aspects of his game and achieved greatness with nary a hit of arrogance or cockiness. The genuineness of his work ethic and attitude remained unquestioned. It led to the following praise expressed by *New York* magazine writer David Amsden in 2007:

> He comes across as so wholesome that you suspect he was frozen sometime around 1955 and thawed out three years ago, when he made his first start at third base in the major leagues. His friends note, almost apologetically, that he is unwaveringly polite and humble and even those who hate him admit that . . . actually, scratch that. No one hates David Wright.[6]

Nobody except opposing pitchers. Wright began 2007 with a 23-game on-base streak, the third-longest in franchise history. The scouting report that indicated how to retire Wright was empty. He hit outside pitches to the opposite field. He pulled inside pitches over the fence. He took his walks when pitched around. And he became a terror on the basepaths, nearly matching his stolen base total from the previous two seasons combined in 2007 with a career-high 34. It could be argued that that was his finest year, one in which he batted .325 and compiled a .416 OBP. His 17-game hitting streak to end that season left him blameless amid the Mets' epic collapse. But one could also claim it was 2008, when he established career-bests in home runs with 33 and RBI with 124.

It certainly wasn't 2009. The puzzling power outage that resulted in just 10 home runs and 72 RBI inspired baseball experts to analyze his mechanics, swing, and approach at the plate, as well as the offensive talent surrounding him. Wright could not be condemned for placing too much emotional and mental load on his back as the Mets descended from one of the best offensive clubs in baseball to among the worst.

The growing number of analytics aficionados were having a field day. Research from Eric Seidman of *Baseball Prospectus* revealed that only five other players in baseball history experienced such a precipitous fall in home run totals after four power-laden seasons, and all were far older than Wright. Nobody knew what to expect in 2010.

Wright provided an inkling on Opening Day. He clobbered a home run to help beat Florida, but more importantly, he began to exhibit the discipline at the plate that allowed him to take his walks and hit the pitches he wanted. Wright took 17 free passes in his first 12 games and exceeded his 2009 home run total by early June, a month in which he raised his batting average from .258 to .311 and drove in 29. He finished the season with 29 homers and 103 RBI. One could no longer argue that the Mets' failures offensively were due greatly to his output. Rather, his output was limited by the lack of productive hitters surrounding him in the lineup.

Soon another factor in the dwindling numbers on his stat line grew evident and would force a permanent decline. Wright had been an iron man through 2010, missing no more than 18 games in any season since 2005. But he injured himself trying to make a diving tag at third in late-April 2011. He was asked by the team to get an MRI for what he believed to be a mild hamstring pull, but it felt better with rest, and he chose to play through the pain, which soon returned and spread to his hips and lower back. He then agreed to an MRI that revealed a stress fracture in his lower back. The issue had certainly affected his performance —he was batting just .205 when placed on the disabled list for the first time in his career.

Wright rebounded to enjoy a very Wright-like season in 2012, batting .306 with 93 RBI. But shoulder and hamstring problems landed him on the DL several times over the next few years. Any hopes for a complete recovery and return to greatness were obliterated in early 2015, when he reinjured his hamstring on a slide and was soon thereafter diagnosed with lumbar spinal stenosis, which causes agonizing muscle and nerve pain in the lower back. He returned to play 38 games that year but struggled in the playoffs and World Series. A herniated disc in his neck limited his 2016 season, and related shoulder problems wiped out 2017.

His career was over. He had worked passionately to return to the field, but his physical problems would not allow it. The Mets honored him with two at-bats and a night of his own on September 29, 2018. A sellout crowd of nearly 44,000 fans crammed Citi Field despite their team having faded from the race in May. And Wright expressed thanks to them for embracing him as one of their own. "You guys welcomed me, a 21-year-old kid from Virginia," he said. "You welcomed me as a New Yorker."

Wright added that he had given all he could to the fans and the sport. "I've always tried to picture myself in the stands or picture a kid watching me play for the first time in the stands, and tried to play the game the right way," he said. "If there's a kid in the stands that is looking for a player to emulate like I used to as a young kid, I wanted to be that player."

Choking back tears, Wright encapsulated the feelings he had for the fans that had always been reciprocated. "Words can't express my gratitude and appreciation for always having my back," he said. "This is love. I can't say anything else. This is love."[7]

Injuries had derailed his path to Cooperstown. But that love was a two-way street. It would never diminish in his heart nor in those of the fans who loved him back.

CHAPTER NINETEEN

New Manager, New GM, New Park in New York

A SENSE OF CHANGE PERMEATED THE METS ORGANIZATION HEADING into the 2005 season. Ownership had hired a new manager (Willie Randolph) and new general manager (Omar Minaya). The infusion of minority leadership for the first time in team history certainly felt novel. And discussions revolving around ditching Shea Stadium to build a ballpark that would tie an old-school atmosphere with modern conveniences promised a fresh feel for the future.

The club on the field, however, could still have been called the New York Mess the previous two seasons. The stated desire to imbue the roster with young standouts had not yet come to fruition despite the promising presence of David Wright and José Reyes. The pitching staff was filled with fading pitchers in their mid-thirties and beyond. The team had lost an average of 93 games under Art Howe in 2003 and 2004.

If the Mets did not boast the talent in their farm system to transform themselves into a contender, at least they could upgrade their stable of veterans. That is what Minaya did in his first off-season. He allowed oldsters such as starting pitcher Al Leiter, relievers John Franco and Ricky Bottalico, and third baseman Todd Zeile and their average age of 38 to walk in free agency. He traded 37-year-old left-hander Mike Stanton to the Yankees.

But rather than risk further regression by committing to a youth movement, Minaya began spending big bucks on veteran superstars. The

Former Yankees second-base standout Willie Randolph is seen here surveying his surroundings during his run as Mets manager from 2005 to 2008.

General Manager Omar Minaya aided the process as the Mets grew into title contenders in the mid-2000s.

**Carlos Beltrán managed three of his finest seasons after signing a
free-agent contract with the Mets in 2005.**

first splash in early January marked the arrival of offensive juggernaut Carlos Beltrán, for whom they outbid the Yankees and Astros. The Mets forked over a franchise-record $119 million over seven years to land a badly needed run producer in the outfield. Beltrán had averaged 29 home runs and 103 RBI over the previous four seasons while emerging as one of the premier base-stealing threats in baseball—he had swiped a career-high 42 in 2004.

Minaya spoke about his motivation at a press conference attended by about 250 media members. "I think the biggest factor is we were tired of losing," he said. "We wanted a new face for the team. We wanted to retool."[1]

Some expected Minaya to follow up by landing first baseman Carlos Delgado, who instead took his power bat to Miami. The Mets opted for far less pricy and far less talented Doug Mientkiewicz, whose weak hitting, especially for that position, inspired Minaya to trade for Delgado a year later.

But the new GM had already begun stocking the 2005 roster with veteran superstars. Splash #1 was 33-year-old future Hall of Fame right-hander Pedro Martínez, who had displayed Koufax-esque dominance for Montreal and Boston, shutting down one hitter after another in the midst of the steroid era while winning five ERA titles and thrice leading the league in strikeouts. He had lost some velocity and late bite on his breaking pitches the previous season in Boston but he still boasted the fierce competitive spirit that had marked his career, and the Mets banked on him remaining a quality starter to the tune of $53 million over four years.

Martínez claimed the lucrative contract was secondary in his decision to leave Boston for the Big Apple. "I was a millionaire at 24," he said. "When I got to Boston, I made millions. You didn't pick up a bum from the street. It was more of a commitment for a team than it was for money. I gave Boston every opportunity for three years to keep me. Boston wouldn't pull the trigger."[2]

Minaya had added just $4 million to the payroll even after those expensive signings. And the result was sterling in 2005 despite a disappointing year from Beltrán. A renaissance year from Cliff Floyd, who smashed a career-high 34 home runs and drove in 98 at age 33, offset the lack of production from Beltrán, who certainly made up for it in 2006. A rejuvenated Martínez emerged as the ace of the staff with a 15-8 record and devastating 0.949 WHIP (walks and hits to inning pitched). And lefty Tom Glavine belied his 39 years of age with one last, strong campaign. The Mets hung around the periphery of the division race, pulling to within four games of the NL East lead with a 68-60 record in late August before a 3-15 stretch doomed them to watching the playoffs from home. But a 12-4 finish provided hope for the future. So appreciative were the fans that 47,718 crammed Shea Stadium to watch the season finale.

Randolph and the front office understood they were headed in the right direction. They perceived accurately that the club needed only a couple of major additions to patch holes. Among them was one more power bat in the lineup, so Minaya put on a ski mask in late November and robbed the Marlins of Delgado in a deal that required only the departure of minor-league prospects, including promising first baseman Mike Jacobs. None made a major impact. The swap united Delgado with his buddy Carlos Beltrán, a fellow Puerto Rican who he said eagerly would serve as his personal guide to New York.

The other desperate need was a lockdown closer, so five days later, the GM pulled out his wallet and signed dominant left-hander Billy Wagner, whose smallish size masked a wicked fastball responsible for a career average of 12 strikeouts per nine innings and eight All-Star Game appearances. Unlike most closers with a short shelf life, Wagner was 34 and still mowing them down. He proved himself worthy of every penny of his four-year, $43 million deal.

The Mets pursued Wagner more aggressively than the competition. The offer of a fourth year and a no-trade clause in the contract proved vital. So did the lure of an unusual and unexpected source. And that was Mets director of corporate services James Plummer, who was raised in a rural village in the highlands of southwestern Virginia a mere 30 miles from Wagner's hometown of Tannersville. The two chatted, and it was revealed Plummer knew Wagner's uncle, which extended the conversation to a half-hour. "These two guys are just talking about just country boy stuff," Minaya recalled. "Going over the second mountain and making a left, and I'm listening to all this and don't know what it means. But I think it made Billy feel comfortable."[3]

Along with Delgado, the further addition through another rip-off of the rebuilding Marlins of viable catcher Paul Lo Duca, who was about to embark on his finest season, and free-agent signing of power-hitting veteran shortstop Jose Valentin more than made up for the loss of Piazza.

Meanwhile, something more far-reaching was brewing in Flushing. Mayor Michael Bloomberg and New York governor George Pataki three days into the regular season unveiled designs for a new ballpark that would open in 2009 in what was then the parking lot between Shea Stadium and 126th Street. The goal was to create a venue that would combine the state-of-the-art amenities of modern stadiums with the old-school atmosphere of classic parks such as Ebbets Field. "Our new

Billy Wagner was a smallish closer but he could really fire the fastball.
WIKIMEDIA COMMONS

ballpark is the realization of a dream—to create a world class environment and enduring experience for everyone, especially for the best fans in all of sports," offered Wilpon. "This new ballpark will become the home our fans have long deserved, one created for shared celebrations among future generations of Mets fans."[4] That ballpark would eventually be known as Citi Field.

Future plans soon gave way to present achievements. The 2006 offense proved itself arguably the most potent in Mets history. They scored 112 more runs than the 2005 edition and blasted 200 over the fence. Out to verify his first year with the team was an anomaly, Beltrán tied Todd Hundley's single-season franchise home run record with 41 and established a new mark with 127 runs scored. Delgado followed up his brilliant season with another, clubbing 38 out of the park as he, Beltrán, and Wright combined for 346 RBI. Reyes batted .300 with 64 stolen bases and 122 runs scored, and Lo Duca shocked one and all by hitting .318.

The Mets were not only an offensive powerhouse, but Wagner also solidified a lights-out bullpen that overcame a mediocre season from a

Citi Field provided the Mets a new home in 2009.
WIKIMEDIA COMMONS

fading Martínez and an average rotation. Right-handed side-arming vet-eran Chad Bradford, 2001 draftee Aaron Heilman, and emerging Pedro Feliciano and Duaner Sánchez, whom the Mets received in a trade with the Dodgers, all teamed up to shut down foe after foe in close games.

The result was a 97-65 record that tied the crosstown Yankees for the best record in baseball. The Mets ran roughshod over the mediocre National League East, taking over first place in the second game of the season and remaining on top the rest of the year. They achieved an eight-game winning streak on the road against Los Angeles, Arizona, and second-place Philadelphia in early June, during which they averaged 8.7 runs, raised their lead to 9½ games, and coasted from there.

Despite losing Martínez to a season-ending injury, the Mets took their momentum and ran with it against the Dodgers in a three-game sweep of the Division Series. They hit just two home runs as they simply singled and walked their opponent into oblivion. Among the offensive heroes was late-August outfield acquisition Shawn Green, who was nearing the end of a tremendous career. Meanwhile, Wagner contin-ued his dominance by closing out all three games and saving two. A series-clinching battering of old nemesis Greg Maddux, who had beaten the Mets more than any other team in his Hall of Fame career, added the cherry on top.

The surprising elimination of the Yankees by Detroit in the ALDS destroyed any hope of another Subway Series. But it certainly had Minaya crowing. "All I know," he said, "is that the only thing they'll be talking about in the city of New York for the remainder of this season is National League baseball."[5]

That conversation lasted a while as they engaged plucky St. Louis in a seven-game marathon. The Mets were forced to wait five days until that club finished off an upset of San Diego in which they allowed just six runs in four games.

And they were ready when the Cardinals arrived at Shea Stadium. The expected heroes were heroes indeed in a 2-0 victory. Ace Tom Glavine performed as if in his peak years, pitching seven shutout innings. Wagner hurled a shutout frame for another save. And Beltrán provided the only runs needed with a two-run homer in the sixth inning.

Some believed at that point the Cardinals, who won just 83 games to take the terrible NL Central, would be easy pickings for the powerful Mets. But they indicated otherwise in a come-from-behind 9-6 victory at Shea in Game 2. They showed they were in this battle to stay. And they proved Wagner mortal by battering him for three runs on four hits in the ninth to break a 6-6 tie.

Given a rotation that already lacked depth, the loss of Martínez was already proving problematic for the Mets in this series. They boasted little beyond Glavine. The likes of John Maine, Steve Trachsel, and Óliver Pérez were no match for a Cardinals club that had awoken offensively after a sleepy NLDS. And when they even delivered a knockout of Glavine after four innings in a Game 5 victory, the Mets were on the verge of elimination heading back to Shea.

They needed a gem from Maine and got one for 5⅓ innings before a sellout crowd of 56,334. The Mets defeated NL Cy Young Award winner Chris Carpenter and survived Game 6 despite a two-run ninth against the suddenly shaky Wagner, then received another fine performance from Pérez the next night. Game 7 was a nail-biter. The teams headed into the ninth tied at 1-1. The Cardinals catcher slugged a two-run homer off Heilman to place his team on the verge of the pennant, but singles by Valentin and Endy Chávez in the bottom of the inning gave the Mets hope.

That is when Randolph made a bold move. He pinch-hit for Heilman with limping Cliff Floyd, who had been injured throughout the series. Randolph was hoping for an historic moment such as the legendary blast by hobbling Kirk Gibson in Game 1 of the 1988 Fall Classic, but he got a strikeout instead. And when Beltrán fanned on a nasty curve by Adam Wainwright with the bases loaded, it was over. The Mets could not ride the best record in baseball to an ultimate championship.

But if owner Fred Wilpon or Minaya were shedding tears, they were tears of pride for what their team had accomplished through adversity. The two met in the clubhouse and shared a hug. "The players didn't cheat you, they didn't cheat you," Wilpon told his GM.

It appeared they hadn't cheated them in 2007 either when they owned a 2½ game lead on second-place Philadelphia with seven games remaining, and six against the lowly Nationals and Marlins and all at home. Crowds averaging 50,000 packed Shea Stadium night after night to watch an epic collapse, particularly of the starting pitchers.

Some believed before the season that Minaya was inviting disaster by failing to bolster an aging rotation that lacked depth, opting instead as his major move the replacement of free-agent Cliff Floyd with 40-year-old Moisés Alou, who lost three months to a quadriceps injury but led the team with a career-high .341 batting average. But the starters performed well enough to keep the Mets in first place nearly the entire season.

Then disaster. The Mets allowed 32 runs in a three-game sweep by Washington. And they surrendered 15 more in two defeats by Florida, the second of which featured a seven-run mashing of Glavine in the first inning that knocked them out of the playoffs. The ace southpaw had given up 13 runs in 5⅓ innings in two losses to end the year. And he would never pitch another game in a Mets uniform.

"It's just a tough lesson in baseball," Randolph said. "When you have the opportunity to seal the deal and you don't capitalize, it can come back to haunt you. It's going to be a tough winter."[6]

Randolph would not be around for another tough winter in 2008. He was fired after the Mets fell to 34-35 in mid-June that year despite the contributions of ace left-hander Johan Santana, who had arrived in a trade from Minnesota and finished the season 16-7 with a league-best 2.53 ERA (though he performed far better after Randolph left). An understanding that Minaya was considering his dismissal motivated Randolph to force his hand. Disgruntled fans had been chanting "Fire Willie" during home games and expressed identical sentiments on radio sports talk shows. But though Randolph prodded Minaya to pull the plug or give him a vote of confidence, the skipper claimed shock when the GM gave him the bad news. "I'm really stunned by it," he said. "I (had) actually asked him. I said, 'Omar, do this now. If you're going to do this, do this now. I know you've got a lot of pressure on you, but if I'm not the guy to lead this team then don't let me get on this plane [heading on a West Coast trip].'"[7]

The Mets were fortunate to boast an experienced replacement in bench coach Jerry Manuel, who had won American League Manager of the Year in 2000 with the White Sox. And he wasted little time righting the ship. The team stumbled around for a couple of weeks before soaring on a 10-game winning streak in early July that catapulted them into a tie for first place in the NL East. The pitching staff that had proven maddeningly inconsistent found its groove in the run. The Mets pitched four shutouts and allowed four total runs during one six-game stretch.

A 10-1 blitz in August and steady winning thereafter placed the Mets 3½ games up approaching mid-September and on the verge of another division crown. But though the 2008 collapse proved longer and a bit less stunning than that of the previous year, it remains painful in the hearts and minds of those affected. A 7-10 finish while the Phillies sizzled sent the Mets home early. Crowds of 50,000-plus packed Shea night after night down the stretch to watch their team blow another playoff opportunity and say goodbye to an old home. A loss to Florida on the final day put the final nail in the coffin, wiping out wild card hopes.

David Wright, who had raked with the playoffs at stake, refused to provide any alibis for a team that had lost a spot on the final day of the season for the second year in a row. "We failed," he stated bluntly. "We failed as a team. There's no pointing fingers. There's no excuses. We as a unit did not get the job done."[8]

An era of optimism was over. One of misery was about to begin.

Chapter Twenty

New Home, Bad Baseball, and a Surprise

With every defeat in the sad summer of 2009, the novelty of watching the Mets in their new digs at Citi Field drained away. A promising start before crowds that packed the new ballpark as the weather warmed degenerated suddenly and permanently. With his roster decimated by injuries, Jerry Manuel simply could not stop the bleeding in his first full season as Mets manager. The same players that had powered the club into title contention the previous three years began falling one by one, victims of aging and bad luck.

Not that the 2009 season proved disastrous from the first pitch. The club rolled merrily along early. Despite several flubs by young outfielder Daniel Murphy that turned victory into defeat and precipitated his move to first base, a torrid May sent them soaring into first place with a 27-20 record. They remained over .500 and in the heat of the race in a weak division into late June.

But by then, injuries were taking a toll. Sparkplug shortstop José Reyes hurt his calf in mid-May and was out for the year. Hip surgery had already sidelined Carlo Delgado for the season. Reliever and former Seattle stud J. J. Putz, who was snagged in a deal as a setup man to closer and fellow off-season acquisition Francisco Rodríguez, tore up his elbow in early June and was also finished. A week later starting pitcher John Maine was shut down for the year with a shoulder problem. Other injuries followed, including the icing on a terrible-tasting cake when ace Johan Santana underwent elbow surgery in late August. The Mets collapsed under the weight of the spate, awful defense, and weak pitching.

Daniel Murphy hit for average for the Mets from 2011 to 2015 but did not find his power stroke until joining the Nationals.

They lost 41 of 59 games down the stretch to finish 70-92. Add in the Wilpon family loss of $700 million in its unwitting involvement in the scheme hatched by jailed hedge fund manager Bernie Madoff and the Mets could not wait to put 2009 behind them.

The following year proved little better, especially for Minaya. He had made a splash as a belated Christmas present to his fans before the season, signing free-agent left fielder Jason Bay, who was coming off a 117-RBI season in Boston that placed him seventh in the American League Most Valuable Player voting. The arrival of the slugger about to earn $66 million over four years was met with great fanfare. But Bay bombed. Moving from the cozy confines of Fenway Park to spacious Citi Field, a pitcher's park indeed until the club moved the fences in both in 2011 and 2014, helped destroy his production. Bay, who played hard and made nary an excuse for his struggles, failed to blast one out until mid-April and had just six home runs (amazingly hitting two in one game twice along the way) on July 25. Injuries then ended his season.

Perhaps the worst free-agent signing in Mets history, Bay never recovered as a productive player. And another under-.500 mark played a significant role in costing Manuel and Minaya their jobs. Never mind that the latter had also made a shrewd trade with Texas before that year that landed veteran knuckleballer R. A. Dickey, who would emerge as an ace and even win an NL Cy Young Award in 2012.

Not that Minaya was complaining. He talked as if he might have fired himself if given an objective choice. "I think we needed a change here," he said. "And I spoke to Fred and to [chief operating officer Jeff Wilpon] about this. The bottom line is we had three years where we didn't finish the job. . . . You look at our payroll—they've given me the payroll to go out there and get the job done."[1]

A replacement search outside the organization landed 63-year-old Sandy Alderson, who had served in the same capacity with Oakland and toiled as CEO with San Diego. Alderson eventually had to slash the player budget considerably, then overcame those challenges by trading for and developing young talent in what had been a nearly dormant farm system. One exception to the new miserly policy was the signing of Wright to a seven-year, $138 million contract extension in

December 2012 that proved disastrous given the injuries that would destroy his career.

The first order of business for Alderson was promoting to the managerial role feisty Terry Collins, who had been toiling in the minor-league organization. Collins guided winning clubs in Houston and Anaheim in the 1990s but could not take them to the playoffs. He was given far more rope by the Mets than had previous managers. The club showed patience in its youth movement over the next several years. Its payroll dropped from $132 million in 2010 to $93 million to $73 million in 2013. But though contention proved merely a pipe dream early in his tenure, Collins continued to manage competitive clubs.

The hiring of Collins coincided with the addition of analytics guru Paul DePodesta to Alderson's staff as vice president of player development and amateur scouting. DePodesta had planned to hire Collins as manager of the Dodgers five years earlier but lost that opportunity when he was canned as GM during the interview process. He had not forgotten about Collins, whom he believed would prove an ideal fit as the Mets launched their youth movement and was considered "an absolute star in player development" and "a tremendous organizational guy."[2]

Collins inherited a club seeking to meld mediocre young talent in with mostly mediocre veterans. The plan was especially evident on the pitching staff as prospects such as Dillon Gee and Jon Niese, neither of whom developed into frontline starters, joined the rotation. Meanwhile, fellow prospects like Lucas Duda and Murphy, who didn't blossom into stardom until leaving New York for Washington in free agency in 2016, began receiving significant playing time as well.

More kids arrived and were accompanied by veteran trade and lower-paid free-agent acquisitions. Promising pitchers such as Matt Harvey and Zack Wheeler debuted in 2013. Catcher Travis D'Arnaud assumed the starting spot in 2014. Stud right-hander Jacob deGrom joined the rotation that same year. And when the Mets did decide to blow big bucks, it backfired and provided a reminder of its riskiness. They signed former Tigers and Yankees all-star outfielder Curtis Granderson to a four-year, $60 million deal before the 2014 season, but though he provided leadership and performed well in the 2015 postseason, he failed to produce the

Star right-hander Jacob deGrom prepares to fire in 2015 after winning National League Rookie of the Year honors the previous season.

Matt Harvey faded badly after a promising start with the Mets in the early-to-mid 2010s.

power he had shown across town and fanned far too often for a leadoff hitter. Ancient right-hander Bartolo Colón came a bit cheaper, however, and did manage three strong years.

The immediate result for Collins was, at best, mediocrity. The Mets finished 74-88 in both of his first two seasons at the helm as fans stayed away in droves from Citi Field. They added five to their victory total in 2014 but fewer fans showed up that year as the club ranked thirteenth among 15 in National League attendance. Optimism heading into the following season seemed based only on the incredibly gifted young mound quartet of deGrom, emerging Noah Syndergaard, and lights-out closer Jeurys Familia and Harvey, who was set to rebound from Tommy John surgery. Nobody expected what was to come.

The Nationals arrived at spring training the overwhelming favorite to win the NL East. Indeed, only one in 88 voters among so-called ESPN experts picked the Mets to snag the division. And though some minds might have changed when they reeled off 11 straight victories in April, the old chestnut about baseball seasons being marathons, not sprints, appeared quite appropriate when they followed with a 23-34 stretch that ended in seven straight losses and a 36-37 mark in late June. They hung around .500 into late July but remained just two games back in a division that proved far more winnable than expected.

That's when Alderson pulled off a gem. He swapped two prospects, including highly touted starting pitcher Michael Fulmer, to Detroit for power-hitting outfielder Yoenis Céspedes, who helped transform the offense into a juggernaut. The Mets started scoring in bunches and embarking on tears. They won seven straight games upon his arrival, including a sweep of Washington at Citi Field that forged a tie for the top. They matched that streak later in August by averaging a ridiculous 10.3 runs per game and scoring 49 during one mind-blowing four-game stretch. Then they put the Nationals away with a three-game sweep on the road in early September in which Céspedes smashed three doubles and two home runs among his six hits and drove home seven. Familia saved all three victories as the Mets opened up a seven-game gap, won five more in a row, and coasted to the crown.

Noah Syndergaard provided depth to a strong Mets rotation but was forced to battle through injuries.
WIKIMEDIA COMMONS

Céspedes was batting .432 with six home runs in September as he celebrated his dominance of Washington. Teammate Kelly Johnson, who aided in the final victory with a game-tying home run, conjured up a couple legends in marveling at what Céspedes had accomplished. "When guys with this much talent get on these kinds of rolls, it's unbelievable," he said. "It's so much fun to watch. It really does kind of remind you of some throwback player, like your dad used to tell you about [Roberto] Clemente or [Mickey] Mantle."[3]

The bats went cold over the last week of the regular season, and the Mets lost 11 of 18 after clinching. Meanwhile, National League Division

Series foe Los Angeles sizzled, finishing 25-14. But momentum meant little in a matchup of deep, talented starting rotations and a battle of premier closers in Familia and dynamite Dodgers wipeout artist Kenley Jansen. The experience of right-left knockout punches Zack Greinke and Clayton Kershaw, who finished 2-3 in the Cy Young Award voting, seemed to give LA the edge in starting pitching in a best-of-five series.

But deGrom outpitched them both in head-to-head battles. He fired seven shutout innings with 13 strikeouts in a Game 1 defeat of Kershaw for one of the greatest playoff performances in major-league history. And in a decisive Game 5, he outperformed Greinke, blanking the Dodgers for five innings after allowing two in the first. Murphy played the role of offensive hero with a homer and double, and Familia did the rest. The Mets had advanced to the NLCS against Chicago, which had already dispatched St. Louis.

The Cubs were not only the sentimental favorite, having failed to win a World Series since 1908. They were also the betting favorite to beat New York. One could certainly have imagined the Mets winning. But nobody could have dreamed how it played out. The quartet of Harvey, Syndergaard, deGrom, and emerging Steven Matz, as well as a bullpen led by Familia, held a strong Cubs lineup to just eight runs in a stunning four-game sweep. Chicago batted .164 in the series and compiled a .225 on-base percentage.

Meanwhile, Murphy rose to the occasion again with nine hits, including, amazingly, one home run in every game. He had slugged one out six games in a row to establish a major-league postseason record. He was blossoming before the eyes of the nation. And so were the young Mets, who returned to the field after celebrating in the clubhouse to share the joy with their home fans. The throng still remained to chant the names of their favorite players and cheer. And perhaps the man who most appreciated the outpouring was a philosophical Wright, who had experienced the best and the worst of Mets baseball since joining the organization 14 years earlier. "This is a long time coming," he said. "I'm glad that I got a chance to kind of experience some of the misery with them along this road, because that champagne tastes a lot sweeter having gone through that, let me tell you."[4]

Matz of the Mets: Steven Matz struggled to establish himself as a consistent stand-out in the late 2010s.

There would be no more champagne. World Series opponent Kansas City proved a different animal. Its lone standout strength was a deep, lockdown bullpen. But the Royals were also tough outs. They fanned the fewest times in the American League and were not overpowered by Mets pitching as were the Dodgers and Cubs. Rather it was the Mets' bats that fell silent—even Murphy managed just three hits in 20 at-bats.

The key inning of the series proved to be the eighth in Game 4. The Mets had won the previous battle and appeared on the verge of tying the series. But the bullpen turned a 3-2 lead into a 5-3 defeat. Then Collins gave his relievers no chance to shut down the Royals in Game 5 after Harvey had hurled eight shutout innings and taken a 2-0 lead into the ninth. Cameras caught the young right-hander imploring his manager to let him try closing it out. Collins acceded to the demand despite Harvey having exceeded 100 pitches and the task of facing the heart of the Kansas City order for the fourth time looming. A walk and run-scoring double followed. Soon, the game was tied. Right-hander Addison Reed, who had performed well after his late-season acquisition, allowed five runs in the twelfth. Season over. Collins was left to lament his mistake. "I let my heart get in the way of my gut," he said about his fatal refusal to remove Harvey.[5]

The pain of losing a World Series never goes away. But there was less of it for the Mets in 2015. Few expected them to contend for the playoffs, let alone compete in the Fall Classic. Indeed, the sky seemed to be the limit for a team with the most dominant young pitching in baseball. But it would not take long for the sky to fall and take the Mets along with it.

CHAPTER TWENTY-ONE

The Sky Fell

JACOB DEGROM. MATT HARVEY. NOAH SYNDERGAARD. ZACK WHEELER.
Steven Matz. Jeurys Familia. The names read like a scary warning to the
rest of the National League. That is, the Mets were destined to dominate.

But this was not the era of Seaver, Koosman, and Ryan. It was a
time of split-finger fastballs, wicked sliders, Tommy John surgeries, and
shortened careers. Eventually, a Mets rotation with so much promise was
reduced by injury, poor performance, free agency, and trade to one super
starter and one maybe.

The first to fall was Harvey, who appeared to have rebounded quite
well from the dreaded Tommy John surgery in 2015 with his mid-90s
fastball and sharp-breaking slider that resulted in a 2.71 ERA and a
strikeout per inning. Super-shark agent Scott Boras suggested that he
skip the playoffs over fear of wearing out his arm or even injury, but the
stakes were far too large.

One could not claim his heavy usage in the postseason played a role
in what happened next. But Harvey had lost some velocity by Opening
Day 2016. His mechanics became flawed trying to compensate, and
after successive poundings, he landed on the disabled list in early July
with what was diagnosed as thoracic outlet syndrome. He opted for
season-ending surgery, returned to pitch well early in 2017, then fell
apart. Harvey earned a three-game suspension for failing to show up to
Citi Field for a game, pitched horribly over his next seven starts, then
returned to the disabled list with a stress fracture to his scapula. He came
back in September but perhaps wished he had not after compiling a

disturbing 11.28 ERA and allowing an absurd 58 baserunners over 22⅓ innings. By early May 2018, he was on his way to Cincinnati.

Though Matz did not fall that far and remained a viable starter through 2019, his upside certainly required revision as well. The southpaw had continued to show vast potential as a rookie in 2016 after flashing brilliance the year before. But left shoulder problems halted his season in August, then an elbow injury that required surgery caused a further setback. He pitched well early in his 2017 comeback before falling apart and raising his ERA from 2.12 to 6.08 over just eight starts. Matz rebounded as a decent rotation contributor over the next two years but one could only guess if he would ever achieve much beyond mediocrity.

Wheeler was forced to climb a higher mountain than Matz. He lost 2015 and 2016 to Tommy John. He struggled to find his groove upon his return to start the 2017 season, then performed well for a month until allowing 15 earned runs over 3 ⅔ innings in back-to-back starts against Chicago and Los Angeles in late June that preceded a short stay on the disabled list for biceps tendinitis. After four more bad outings, he was placed again on the DL with a stress reaction in his right arm and was out for the year. Wheeler rebounded in 2018 and 2019 to pitch well, though not dominantly, then hightailed it to Philadelphia in free agency.

Meanwhile, Syndergaard emerged as the Mets' premier pitcher aside from deGrom. But he too was forced to fight tough battles beyond those against batters. He arrived at camp in 2017 firing his fastball at nearly 100 miles per hour. The man respectfully nicknamed Thor had in 2016 compiled a 14-9 record with 218 strikeouts in 183⅔ innings and led the National League in fewest home runs allowed per inning. Perhaps he felt invincible when he refused to undergo an MRI after missing a start with biceps tendinitis. He tore his lat (latissimus dorsi muscle) in his next outing and missed five months, returning only to pitch three innings. A sore index finger knocked him out for six weeks in 2018. Syndergaard performed well upon his return, then took a step back in 2019, leading the league in earned runs allowed. Then came the crowning blow in March 2020, when he too was determined to require Tommy John surgery.

The fragility of a pitching career indeed proved itself to all five once-sterling starters. Even deGrom lost the last month of 2016 to a

Zack Wheeler.

triceps injury, though his primary bugaboo eventually proved to be a pronounced lack of run support. The destruction of a once-promising rotation destroyed any hope that the Mets would maintain their status as a contender, let alone the dynasty some believed they could forge based on the dominance of their starters. Offered *New York Post* columnist Larry Brooks in May 2018:

> The end has happened to the dream rotation. As John Greenleaf Whittier once wrote about sad words not so long after Abner Doubleday invented the game, "The saddest are these, it might have been."[1]

What might have been faded into reality, though the Mets managed one last hurrah for the second decade of the twenty-first century in 2016 when a hot September earned them a one-game wild-card playoff against San Francisco that featured an incredible pitcher's duel between Syndergaard and Giants ace Madison Bumgarner. A three-run homer by weak-hitting Conor Gillaspie off Familia in the ninth doomed the Mets, who would spend the rest of that October and the next three on the outside looking in.

The problems developed over those seasons had a familiar ring, especially regarding their position players. The Mets simply failed to produce enough talent from the farm to restock a lineup that had lost David Wright. Veteran stopgaps such as Jay Bruce, Adrián González, Robinson Canó, and Todd Frazier could not fill the void through 2019. Promising prospects such as outfielders Michael Conforto and Pete Alonso, who raised many an eyebrow with his 53-homer Rookie-of-the-Year explosion in 2019, were few and far between.

The lean years produced two managerial victims. The first was Collins, who was given little rope after a 72-90 season in 2017 that followed a World Series and wild card appearance. Collins was fired in favor of Mickey Callaway, who was plucked from Cleveland, where he had been serving as a pitching coach. Collins, however, did not complain. He had been worn out emotionally from a brutal season. "There was a time this summer where I said, 'I'm not sure I can keep doing this,'" said an

Michael Conforto developed into a consistent run producer on a Mets team that struggled to score.
WIKIMEDIA COMMONS

emotional Collins, who added he might not have accepted a contract extension to remain at the helm if offered. "I care about the team, and it was getting tough. They kept falling down, and so did I."[2]

Callaway represented a rare rookie hire for the Mets. The 43-year-old was lauded for his calm and steady approach to the job, as well as a modern analytical approach, but admitted to the pressures of managing in New York. Every move was dissected, so one can only imagine the media and fan reaction when he turned in the wrong lineup card for a game a month into his tenure, wrecking an early rally in a Mets defeat.

A hot start in 2018 was followed by one of the worst runs in franchise history. A 5-22 stretch not only sent the team spiraling out of the race, but it also motivated Sandy Alderson, who was also battling a recurrence of cancer, to resign as general manager. Callaway, however, received kudos for how he was captaining a ship that was sinking like the *Titanic*.

"This is certainly when good managers show their mettle, and I've been very happy with his attitude through this," offered assistant general

Pete Alonso, shown here enjoying the 2019 MLB All-Star parade, exploded onto the scene that year to nearly win National League Most Valuable Player honors.
WIKIMEDIA COMMONS

manager John Ricco in the midst of the collapse. "He's bringing solutions and he's creative. He's trying to tap into all of the resources to help get out of this."[3]

Given such praise one might have assumed Callaway would have remained in place after the club finished strong in 2018 and launched a late playoff run a year later. But given that the Mets boasted a Cy Young Award winner in deGrom and a Rookie of the Year in Alonso, it was determined by CEO Jeff Wilpon and GM Brodie Van Wagenen that the Mets were a playoff-caliber club. So Callaway, who was criticized by Wilpon for his in-game decision-making, was sent packing.

The Mets announced heading into 2020 they would replace Callaway with recently retired outfield standout Carlos Beltrán, who had starred with the club from 2005 to 2011. But he was fired before he could manage a game following the revelation of a cheating scandal he had helped engineer in the last year of his playing career in Houston in 2017.

Though the seasons of mediocrity beyond 2016 cost Collins and Callaway their jobs, and misfortune ended the tenure of Beltrán before it really began, there was hope. There had always been hope for Mets fans ever since the rag-tag teams of the 1960s were transformed suddenly and shockingly into World Series champions at Shea Stadium. And if those Mets could do it, so could the bunch that made Citi Field their home.

Sandy Alderson served as Mets general manager from 2010 to 2018.
WIKIMEDIA COMMONS

NOTES

CHAPTER 1: CONCEPTION AND BIRTH IN THE BIG APPLE

1. Jim McCulley, "Wagner, Shea jubilant over NL's decision." *New York Daily News.* October 19, 1960. https://www.nydailynews.com/sports/baseball/mets/mets-born-nl -votes-return-gotham-62-article-1.2144369.
2. This Great Game, "The Polo Grounds." http://www.thisgreatgame.com/ballparks -polo-grounds.html.
3. Pack Bringley, "This date in Mets history—you . . . you . . . and you . . . you're Mets now." Amazin' Avenue. October 10, 2012. https://www.amazinavenue.com/2012/10/10 /3475932/10-10.

CHAPTER 2: THE WORST DARN TEAM IN HISTORY

1. Leonard Schecter, "Bring back the real Mets." *The Complete Armchair Book of Baseball: An All-Star Lineup Celebrates America's National Pastime.* Edison, NJ: Galahad Books, 1985. 304. https://books.google.com/books?id=NAPaOOrSVywC&pg=PA304&lpg= PA304&dq=casey+stengel+alka+seltzer+commercial&source=bl&ots=TaPfCW_e-Y&sig =ACfU3U1-ViPoF5QyJTNN6oQoyeurf6jeMw&hl=en&sa=X&ved=2ahUKEwjH -vihw-_nAhXXG80KHbcDDWUQ6AEwAHoECAoQAQ#v=onepage&q=casey%20 stengel%20alka%20seltzer%20commercial&f=false.
2. Robert Lipsyte, "Spring of '62: Revisiting the dawn of the Mets." *New York Times.* February 19, 2012. https://www.nytimes.com/2012/02/20/sports/baseball/remembering -the-mets-first-spring-in-1962.html.
3. Gary Livacan, "Charlie Culbertson's walk-off homer has a great connection to old-time baseball and 'Marvelous Marv' Throneberry!" Baseball History Comes Alive. https://www.baseballhistorycomesalive.com/charlie-culbertsons-walk-off-homer-has -great-connection-to-old-time-baseball-and-marlevous-marv-throneberry/.
4. Leonard Schecter, "Bring back the real Mets."
5. Ibid. 311.
6. Jeff Kallman, "'Eight million New Yorkers called him Marvelous Marv." Internet Baseball Writers Association of America. March 5, 2019. https://throneberryfields.com /2019/03/05/eight-million-new-yorkers-called-him-marvelous-marv/.
7. Bruce Watson, "The 'Miracle Mets' of '69 win the World Series." American Heritage. https://www.americanheritage.com/node/133061.

Chapter 3: Oh Shea Can You See

1. Chris Landers, "Let's remember when Jimmy Piersall celebrated a homer by moonwalking around the bases." MLB.com. November 9, 2016. https://www.mlb.com/cut4/photo-mets-jimmy-piersall-rounds-bases-backwards-after-home-run-c208451608.
2. George Vecsey, "Deconstructing the legend of Choo Choo." *New York Times*. January 23, 2012. https://www.nytimes.com/2012/01/24/sports/baseball/mets-choo-choo-coleman-50-years-later.html.
3. United Press International, "Ex-Met says Stengel falls asleep on bench." *New York Times*. August 7, 1964. https://www.nytimes.com/1964/08/07/archives/exmet-says-stengel-falls-asleep-on-bench.html.
4. Will Anderson, "Carl Willey." Society for American Baseball Research. https://sabr.org/bioproj/person/1cd9a765.

Chapter 4: Tom Terrific

1. Richard Goldstein, "Bing Devine, builder of World Series winners, dies at 90." *New York Times*. January 31, 2007. https://www.nytimes.com/2007/01/31/sports/baseball/31devine.html.
2. William Leggett, "Tom Seaver: 1969 Sportsman of the Year." *Sports Illustrated*. December 22, 1969. https://vault.si.com/vault/1969/12/22/sportsman-of-the-year.
3. Maxwell Cates, "Tom Seaver." Society for American Baseball Research. https://sabr.org/bioproj/person/486af3ad.
4. John Delcos, "This date in Mets history: Tom Seaver wins Rookie of the Year." Metsmerized Online. November 20, 2013. https://metsmerizedonline.com/2013/11/this-date-in-mets-history-tom-seaver-wins-rookie-of-the-year.html/.
5. William Leggett, "Lights in the Met cellar." *Sports Illustrated*. May 6, 1968. https://vault.si.com/vault/1968/05/06/lights-in-the-met-cellar.
6. Mary Hershberger. *American Peace Activists and the War*. Syracuse, NY: Syracuse University Press, 1998. 100. https://books.google.com/books?id=voXj6erAp4cC&pg=PA100&lpg=PA100&dq=Did+Seaver+call+Vietnam+%22perfectly+ridiculous%22&source=bl&ots=UTpjzrwBGH&sig=ACfU3U2_tZdT0dhIkybdsAWYy_IozyIk3w&hl=en&sa=X&ved=2ahUKEwj8iuP7pqLoAhWYAZ0JHZuMA3gQ6AEwAnoECAsQAQ#v=onepage&q=Did%20Seaver%20call%20Vietnam%20%22perfectly%20ridiculous%22&f=false.
7. Maxwell Kates, "Tom Seaver."
8. Ibid.

Chapter 5: From Chumps to Champs

1. Len Ferman, "Innovative lessons from the Miracle Mets of 1969: Part 1 of 3." Maritz CX. October 29, 2019. https://www.maritzcx.com/blog/general/innovation-lessons-from-the-miracle-mets-of-1969/.
2. Bud Harrelson and Phil Pepe. *Turning Two: My Journey to the Top of the World and Back with the New York Mets*. New York: Thomas Dunne Books, 2012. 63.

3. Matthew Silverman, "Tug McGraw." Society for American Baseball Research. https://sabr.org/bioproj/person/0834272a.

4. Bruce Watson, "The 'Miracle Mets' of '69 win the World Series." American Heritage. https://www.americanheritage.com/node/133061.

5. Steve Jacobson, "Weaver sees eight runs down the drain." *Newsday*. October 15, 1969.

6. Joe Donnelly, "Return trip to Baltimore? It's going to be tough now." *Newsday*. October 15, 1969.

7. Phil Pepe, "Mets refuse to quit, rally to beat the Baltimore Orioles 5-3 in Game 5 at Shea Stadium to win 1969 World Series." *New York Daily News*. October 17, 1969. https://www.nydailynews.com/sports/baseball/mets/mets-beat-orioles-5-3-win-66th -world-series-1969-article-1.2386264.

8. Bruce Markusen, "The miracle remembered: Those '69 Mets." *Hardball Times*. February 14, 2019. https://tht.fangraphs.com/the-miracle-remembered-those-69-mets/.

9. Bruce Watson, "The 'Miracle Mets' of '69 win the World Series."

CHAPTER 6: YOGI AND THE YEARS OF MEDIOCRITY

1. Gary Livacari, "The baseball world mourns the sudden passing of Gil Hodges." Baseball History Comes Alive. April 2, 2019. https://www.baseballhistorycomesalive .com/the-baseball-world-mourns-the-sudden-passing-of-gil-hodges/.

2. Matthew Silverman, "Tug McGraw." Society for American Baseball Research. https://sabr.org/bioproj/person/0834272a.

3. Ibid.

4. Pack Bringley, "Top 50 Mets of all time: #31 Tug McGraw." Amazin Avenue. March 17, 2014. https://www.amazinavenue.com/2014/3/17/5518050/mets-tug-mcgraw-top -50-all-time.

5. Joseph Durso, "Mets in World Series; defeat Reds for flag." *New York Times*. October 11, 1973. https://www.nytimes.com/1973/10/11/archives/mets-in-world-series-defeat -reds-for-flag-mets-defeat-reds-72-for.html.

6. Joseph Durso, "A's top Mets, 5-2, win Series again." *New York Times*. October 22, 1973. https://www.nytimes.com/1973/10/22/archives/a-s-top-mets-52-win-series-again -campaneris-jackson-clout-2run.html.

CHAPTER 7: FROM CONTENTION TO COLLAPSE

1. David E. Skelton, "George Stone," Society for American Baseball Research. https:// sabr.org/bioproj/person/695dab6a.

2. Fred Worth, "Cleon Jones." Society for American Baseball Research. https://sabr.org /bioproj/person/b4f5e5c2.

3. Joseph Durso, "Mets dismiss Berra and name McMillan." *New York Times*. August 7, 1975. https://www.nytimes.com/1975/08/07/archives/mets-dismiss-berra-and-name -mcmillan-5game-losing-streak-led-to.html.

4. Jack Lang, "Mets look up problems still smolder." *Sporting News*. July 10, 1976. 8.

Chapter 8: The Kiddie Corps

1. Ron Fimrite, "No wonder he's hot." *Sports Illustrated*. January 12, 1987. https://vault
.si.com/vault/1987/01/12/no-wonder-hes-hot-just-kidding-mike-scott-was-so-good
-in-86-that-folks-say-he-does-something-to-the-ball.
2. Ray Kerby, "An interview with Mike Scott." Astrosdaily.com. February 4, 2002.
https://www.astrosdaily.com/players/interviews/Scott_Mike.html.
3. Jeff Pearlman. *The Bad Guys Won*. New York: HarperCollins, 2004. 26.
4. Bill Francis, "Davey Johnson's managerial skills lead him to Cooperstown's doorstep."
National Baseball Hall of Fame. https://baseballhall.org/discover-more/news/johnson
-davey.
5. Bruce Weber, "Managing the Mets: The future is now." *New York Times*. March 24,
1985. https://www.nytimes.com/1985/03/24/magazine/managing-the-mets-the-future
-is-now.html.
6. Joseph Durso, "Mets stumble on the threshold of first place." *New York Times*.
October 4, 1985. https://www.nytimes.com/1985/10/04/sports/mets-stumble-on-the
-threshold-of-first-place.html.

Chapter 9: Fighting Greatness

1. Tom Verducci, "Summer of Doc." *Sports Illustrated*. August 2015. https://www.si.com
/longform/2015/1985/doc/index.html.
2. Geoffrey Gray, "Doc's debut." Sports on Earth. April 7, 2014. http://www.sports
onearth.com/article/71220258/thirty-years-ago-dwight-gooden-made-his-first-start
-for-the-mets.
3. Misc. Baseball, "Dwight Gooden in 1983." https://miscbaseball.wordpress.com/
tag/1983-lynchburg-mets/.
4. Joseph Durso, "Gooden's promise unlimited." *New York Times*. September 17, 1984.
https://www.nytimes.com/1984/09/17/sports/gooden-s-promise-unlimited.html.
5. Ibid.
6. Tom Verducci, "Summer of Doc."
7. Ibid.
8. Ibid.
9. Jeff Pearlman. *The Bad Guys Won*. New York: HarperCollins, 2004. 54.
10. Tom Verducci, "From phenom to phantom." *Sports Illustrated*. March 22, 1993.
https://vault.si.com/vault/1993/03/22/from-phenom-to-phantom-a-ghost-of-his-for
mer-self-dwight-gooden-at-28-tries-to-recapture-the-glory-of-his-youth.

Chapter 10: 1986

1. Jeff Pearlman. *The Bad Guys Won*. New York: HarperCollins, 2004. 182.
2. Michael Martinez, "4 Mets arrested in fight." *New York Times*. July 20, 1986. https://
www.nytimes.com/1986/07/20/sports/4-mets-arrested-in-fight.html.
3. Jeff Pearlman. *The Bad Guys Won*. 182.

4. Joseph Durso, "Baseball; Mets win, 6-5, on Dykstra homer." *New York Times*. October 12, 1986. https://www.nytimes.com/1986/10/12/sports/baseball-mets-win-6-5-on
-dykstra-homer.html.

5. Jeff Pearlman. *The Bad Guys Won*. 198.

6. Mike Vaccaro, "The Game 6 the world forgot, but Mets fans never will." *New York Post*. May 23, 2016. https://nypost.com/2016/05/23/the-game-6-the-world-forgot-but
-mets-fans-never-will/.

7. Jeff Pearlman. *The Bad Guys Won*. 204.

8. Joseph Durso, "Mets and Red Sox win their pennants." *New York Times*. October 16, 1986. https://www.nytimes.com/1986/10/16/sports/mets-and-red-sox-win-their
-pennants.html.

9. Jeff Pearlman. *The Bad Guys Won*. 218.

10. Malcolm Moran, "The World Series '86: Nightmare ends Teufel's day of promise." *New York Times*. October 19, 1986. https://www.nytimes.com/1986/10/19/sports/the
-world-series-86-nightmare-ends-teufel-s-day-of-promise.html.

11. Jeff Pearlman. *The Bad Guys Won*. 219.

12. Jeff Pearlman. *The Bad Guys Won*. 241.

13. Peter Alfano, "The World Series '86; Mets win it, city loves it." *New York Times*. October 28, 1986. https://www.nytimes.com/1986/10/28/sports/the-world-series-86
-mets-win-it-city-loves-it.html.

14. Ross Newhan, "Mets: Frustration is forgotten on night of celebration." *Los Angeles Times*. October 28, 1986. https://www.latimes.com/archives/la-xpm-1986-10-28-sp
-8088-story.html.

15. Ibid.

16. Jeff Pearlman. *The Bad Guys Won*. 260.

CHAPTER 11: WHEN GREAT WAS NOT GOOD ENOUGH

1. Ibid. 264.

2. Roger Angell. *A Pitcher's Story*. New York: Warner Books, 2001. 154.

3. Lyle Spencer, "Oral history of epic Mets-Dodgers 1988 NLCS." MLB.com. June 14, 2019. https://www.mlb.com/news/oral-history-of-epic-mets-dodgers-1988-nlcs.

4. Shirley Povich, "An old ghost might've headed Cone off." *Washington Post*. October 9, 1988. https://www.washingtonpost.com/archive/sports/1988/10/09/an-old-ghost
-mightve-headed-cone-off/9f65432e-a127-499f-a39e-c3ea04bb554a/.

5. Lyle Spencer, "Oral history of epic Mets-Dodgers 1988 NLCS."

6. Joseph Durso, "Cone stars as Mets battle their way into Game 7." *New York Times*. October 12, 1988. https://www.nytimes.com/1988/10/12/sports/cone-stars-as-mets
-battle-their-way-into-game-7.html.

7. David Schoenfield, "The most hyped prospect ever for all 30 MLB teams." ESPN. April 9, 2020. https://www.espn.com/mlb/story/_/id/29003518/the-most-hyped-pros
pect-ever-all-30-mlb-teams.

8. Jeff Pearlman. *The Bad Guys Won*. New York: HarperCollins, 2004. 268.

CHAPTER 12: GOODBYE DAVEY, HELLO MISERY

1. Jack Curry, "Johnson dismissed by Mets; Harrelson named manager." *New York Times*. May 30, 1990. https://www.nytimes.com/1990/05/30/sports/johnson-dismissed -by-mets-harrelson-named-manager.html.
2. Eric Aron, "Bud Harrelson." Society for American Baseball Research. https://sabr .org/bioproj/person/cb7f6459.
3. Joe Sexton, "Mets sign Bonilla for $29 million, making him richest in baseball." *New York Times*. December 3, 1991. https://www.nytimes.com/1991/12/03/sports/mets-sign -bonilla-for-29-million-making-him-richest-in-baseball.html.
4. Joe Sexton, "Baseball: It's lights out for Torborg after one last blast; Green is hired to hoist Mets out of cellar." *New York Times*. May 20, 1993. https://www.nytimes.com /1993/05/20/sports/baseball-it-s-lights-for-torborg-after-one-last-blast-green-hired -hoist-mets.html.

CHAPTER 13: THE HOMETOWN CLOSER

1. Hank Hersch, "A hometown hero." *Sports Illustrated*. May 15, 1989. https://vault.si .com/vault/1989/05/15/a-hometown-hero-reliever-john-franco-eats-up-batters-for -cincinnati-but-his-heart-and-stomach-belong-to-brooklyn.
2. John Harper, "John Franco: From St. John's to the NY Mets' Hall of Fame, reliever is a city legend." *New York Daily News*. June 3, 2012. https://www.nydailynews.com /sports/baseball/mets/john-franco-st-john-ny-mets-hall-fame-reliever-city-legend -article-1.1088811.
3. Hank Hersch, "A hometown hero."
4. Tom Friend, "Baseball; Franco looks for a missing ingredient." *New York Times*. September 24, 1993. https://www.nytimes.com/1993/09/24/sports/baseball-franco -looks-for-a-missing-ingredient.html.
5. *The Sporting News*, "Quick hits: Players who provided special postseason moments. Change is eternal: John Franco." October 16, 2000.

CHAPTER 14: VALENTINE'S DAY

1. Alan Cohen, "Bret Saberhagen." Society for American Baseball Research. https:// sabr.org/bioproj/person/8f00b9b0.
2. Murray Chass, "Mets, in move to serve their youth, dismiss Green." *New York Times*. August 27, 1996. https://www.nytimes.com/1996/08/27/sports/mets-in-move-to-serve -their-youth-dismiss-green.html.
3. Buster Olney, "Mets learn to love Valentine: Ex-Spokane star succeeds second time around." *Spokane Spokesman-Review*. June 24, 1997. https://www.spokesman.com/stories /1997/jun/24/mets-learn-to-love-valentine-ex-spokane-star/.
4. Ibid.
5. Jason Diamos, "Baseball; Mets lay their final egg, and it tastes awful." *New York Times*. September 28, 1998. https://www.nytimes.com/1998/09/28/sports/baseball-mets -lay-their-final-egg-and-it-tastes-awful.html.

CHAPTER 15: SUPER SEASON

1. David Waldstein, "Mets ride Ventura highway." *New York Post*. June 30, 1999. https://nypost.com/1999/06/30/mets-ride-ventura-highway/.
2. CBSNews.com, "Mets welcome Rickey Henderson." December 21, 1999. https://www.cbsnews.com/news/mets-welcome-rickey-henderson/.
3. Greg Prince, "The happiest recap: 162-163." Faith and Fear in Flushing. November 2, 2011. http://www.faithandfearinflushing.com/2011/11/02/the-happiest-recap-162-163/.
4. Associated Press, "Alfonzo, Olerud come up big against Unit." ESPN. October 5, 1999. https://www.espn.com/mlb/1999/991005/recap/nymari.html.
5. Judy Battista, "Baseball playoffs: league championships; After 15 pitchers and 15 innings, Mets live." *New York Times*. October 18, 1999. https://www.nytimes.com/1999/10/18/sports/baseball-playoffs-league-championships-after-15-pitchers-15-innings-mets-live.html.
6. Judy Battista, "1999 playoffs: league championships; Subway Series dies hard: Mets lose it all on a walk." *New York Times*. October 20, 1999. https://www.nytimes.com/1999/10/20/sports/1999-playoffs-league-championships-subway-series-dies-hard-mets-lose-it-all-walk.html.

CHAPTER 16: THE SUBWAY SERIES

1. Associated Press, "Phillips: 'Something had to be done.'" ESPN. May 15, 2000. https://www.espn.com/mlb/news/2000/0513/530443.html.
2. Josh Dubrow, "Jones' one-hitter ends Giants' season." Associated Press. October 9, 2000.
3. Associated Press, "Hampton, Mets take World Series stage." October 16, 2000. https://www.espn.com/mlb/2000/20001016/recap/stlnym.html.
4. Rafael Hermoso, "Baseball: Subway Series; Subway Series experience absent from both teams." *New York Times*. October 21, 2000. https://www.nytimes.com/2000/10/21/sports/baseball-subway-series-subway-series-experience-absent-from-both-teams.html.
5. Ibid.
6. Mike Piazza with Lonnie Wheeler, "There should have been a fight." Sports on Earth. February 12, 2013. http://www.sportsonearth.com/article/41538148.
7. Ibid.
8. Wallace Mathews, "Meek the Mets: Piazza, Amazin's have weak response after Clemens goes batty." *New York Post*. October 30, 2000. https://nypost.com/2000/10/30/meek-the-mets-piazza-amazins-have-weak-response-after-clemens-goes-batty/.
9. Buster Olney, "After riveting ride, decisions for a dynasty." *New York Times*. October 28, 2000. http://movies2.nytimes.com/2000/10/28/sports/28YANK.html.
10. Tyler Kepner, "The Mets lose, but their pride is intact." *New York Times*. October 27, 2000. http://movies2.nytimes.com/2000/10/27/sports/27METS.html.

Chapter 17: The End of Valentine's Day—and Howe

1. 9/11 Memorial and Museum, "NYC sports teams visit rescue and recovery workers at Ground Zero." https://www.911memorial.org/connect/blog/nyc-sports-teams-visit -rescue-and-recovery-workers-ground-zero.

2. Associated Press, "Mets pull within 4½ on emotional night." September 21, 2001. https://www.espn.com/mlb/recap?gameId=210921121.

3. Associated Press, "Mets match 14-game streak of 1911 Braves." September 1, 2002. https://africa.espn.com/mlb/preview?gameId=220901121.

4. Jack Curry and Rafael Hermoso, "Mets fire Valentine to close out a dismal season." *New York Times*. October 1, 2002. https://www.nytimes.com/2002/10/01/sports/baseball /mets-fire-valentine-to-close-out-a-dismal-season.html.

5. Ibid.

6. Ibid.

7. Associated Press, "Howe's four-year contract worth $9.4 million." October 29, 2002. https://www.espn.com/mlb/news/2002/1028/1452227.html.

8. Rafael Hermoso, "Mets dismiss general manager Phillips." *New York Times*. June 12, 2003. https://www.nytimes.com/2003/06/12/sports/baseball/mets-dismiss-general -manager-phillips.html.

9. *Jet*, "Longtime Yankees coach Willie Randolph named New York Mets manager." November 22, 2004. 51.

Chapter 18: It's All Wright

1. Paul White, "Mets have the right stuff with Wright at third." *Baseball Digest*. July 2006. 20.

2. Lee Jenkins, "Rolen tries to help Wright prepare for the bad hops." *New York Times*. August 7, 2004. https://www.nytimes.com/2004/08/07/sports/baseball-rolen-tries-to -help-wright-prepare-for-the-bad-hops.html.

3. Ira Berkow, "Baseball: Mets' third baseman is learning to relax." *New York Times*. August 17, 2004. https://www.nytimes.com/2004/08/17/sports/baseball-mets-third -baseman-is-learning-to-relax.html.

4. Frank Lidz, "Prince of the city." *Sports Illustrated*. May 29, 2006. https://vault.si.com /vault/2006/05/29/prince-of-the-city.

5. Associated Press, "Mets sign Wright to six-year, $55 million extension." August 8, 2006. https://www.espn.com/mlb/news/story?id=2541623.

6. David Amsden, "Mr. Clean: He's young! Rich! Handsome! Able to throw out a runner at first base while flashing a killer smile! David Wright is the perfect New York sports star—almost too perfect." *New York*. April 9, 2007. 26.

7. John Delcos, "Why Mets fans will miss David Wright." *Forbes*. September 30, 2018. https://www.forbes.com/sites/johndelcos/2018/09/30/why-i-will-miss-david-wright /#53d5691025c4.

CHAPTER 19: NEW MANAGER, NEW GM, NEW PARK IN NEW YORK

1. Jack Curry, "Beltrán brings great hope to 'new Mets.'" *New York Times*. January 12, 2005. https://www.nytimes.com/2005/01/12/sports/baseball/Beltrán-brings-great-hope-to-new-mets.html.
2. Associated Press, "Pedro says Red Sox waited too long." December 16, 2004. https://www.espn.com/mlb/news/story?id=1947632.
3. Ben Shpigel, "Secret weapon helped Mets in signing Wagner." *New York Times*. November 30, 2005. https://www.nytimes.com/2005/11/30/sports/baseball/secret-weapon-helped-mets-in-signing-wagner.html.
4. NYC.gov, "Mayor Bloomberg, Governor Pataki, and New York Mets unveil design plans for new ballpark." April 6, 2006. https://www1.nyc.gov/office-of-the-mayor/news/104-06/mayor-bloomberg-governor-pataki-new-york-mets-design-plans-new-ballpark#/0.
5. Ben Shpigel, "Mets win bullpen battle to sweep Dodgers." *New York Times*. October 8, 2005. https://www.nytimes.com/2006/10/08/sports/baseball/08nlds.html.
6. Larry Fine, "Mets' collapse ends on 8-1 loss to Marlins." *Reuters*. September 30, 2007. https://www.reuters.com/article/us-baseball-mets-sunday/mets-collapse-ends-on-8-1-loss-to-marlins-idUSN3022766120070930.
7. ESPN, "Mets fire Randolph; Peterson, Nieto also dismissed." June 17, 2008. https://www.espn.com/mlb/news/story?id=3447973.
8. Associated Press, "Another collapse befalls Mets as bullpen allows key homers." September 28, 2008. https://www.espn.com/mlb/recap?gameId=280928121.

CHAPTER 20: NEW HOME, BAD BASEBALL, AND A SURPRISE

1. Adam Rubin, "Omar Minaya not remaining with Mets." ESPN. October 4, 2010. https://www.espn.com/new-york/mlb/news/story?id=5647075.
2. Ibid.
3. Anthony DiComo and Bill Ladson, "Yoenis Sweptcedes: Mets 7 up after DC dagger." MLB.com. September 9, 2015. https://www.mlb.com/news/yoenis-cespedes-homers-as-mets-sweep-nationals/c-148322308.
4. Tyler Kepner, "Mets, team of big shoulders, sweep Cubs to reach World Series." *New York Times*. October 22, 2015. https://www.nytimes.com/2015/10/22/sports/baseball/new-york-mets-beat-chicago-cubs-nlcs.html.
5. Twitter: Phil Taylor. *Sports Illustrated*. https://bleacherreport.com/articles/2585129-for-vanquished-mets-missed-opportunities-will-forever-define-2015-world-series.

Chapter 21: The Sky Fell

1. Larry Brooks, "Harvey's exit nail in the coffin to Mets' projected dream rotation." *New York Post*. May 5, 2018. https://nypost.com/2018/05/05/harveys-exit-nail-in-the-coffin-to-mets-projected-dream-rotation/.

2. James Wagner, "Terry Collins will stay with the Mets, but not as manager." *New York Times*. October 1, 2017. https://www.nytimes.com/2017/10/01/sports/baseball/terry-collins-mets-fired.html.

3. James Wagner, "Mickey Callaway, Mets' rookie manager, shows veteran's calm amid skid." *New York Times*. May 14, 2018. https://www.nytimes.com/2018/05/14/sports/mickey-callaway-mets.html.

Printed in Great Britain
by Amazon